The Found World of Quintana Roo

The Found World of Quintana Roo

A 600 MILE TREK OFF THE BEATEN PATH

• • •

Wendy Morrill
Section Maps Illustrated by Debra Tall, copyright 2012
Edited by Amanda Husson

ISBN: 1540754030
ISBN 13: 9781540754035
Library of Congress Control Number: 2016921341
CreateSpace Independent Publishing Platform
North Charleston, South Carolina

Off the Beaten Path

"The ordinary traveller, who never goes off the beaten route and who on this beaten route is carried by others [ie. guide], without himself doing anything or risking anything, does not need to show much more initiative and intelligence than an express package."

Theodore Roosevelt, 1913.

For Dad
You made my dreams come true.

Prologue

• • •

While making our way to Akumal in the early afternoon, we encountered one of our biggest obstacles: a large remote inlet about 200 feet in width. The seawater was too deep to wade across. At the far end of the inlet, there were too many swamps and mangroves to walk around. Besides, that would have added more distance to our journey. There were no people or settlements with boats nearby to ask for help.

My father declared, "We need to make a raft!"

"*What?*" I exclaimed, and my heart started beating faster.

We looked around the jungle to see what material was available to construct this rudimentary Tom Sawyer raft...

CHAPTER 1

Background: A Lifetime of Adventures with Dad

• • •

AFTER READING *THE LOST WORLD of Quintana Roo* by Michael Peissel, I realized that the soft white sandy beach runs the entire length of the Caribbean Yucatán. I also realized that almost no major rivers interrupt the flow of the shoreline. Unlike most of the vacationers who stay at the Cancún resorts and who may not venture off the properties, I thought that walking the entire coastline would be thrilling. I called my dad to share my idea, and grinning from ear to ear, I said, "Dad, we should walk from Cancún to Belize."

Of course, he asked, "When do you want to leave?"

I always dreamed of planning an expedition in a third world tropical country. But I needed training. And who better to train me in adventuring off the beaten path than my dad?

I live for traveling and sharing these experiences with others, and I love the excitement of the unknown, cultural anthropology, and education. I only fear two things in this world: black spiders and dark basements. Black spiders make me scream like a little girl, and they give me the heebie-jeebies. When I was a seaman in the United States Navy, I stood on the weather deck of a steel diving boat one morning, and I found a spider with a diameter of three inches crawling along my leg. I moved so quickly that I almost fell overboard. Dark basements with many hiding places also frighten me because I have watched too many horror movies as a child, particularly movies like *The Amityville Horror*. My father scolded me as a kid when he and my mom would come home after date night and I had allowed the woodstove fire to go out because I was too afraid to venture downstairs and put logs in it.

However, if you put me in a foreign place, I will feel right at home. All of my senses come alive. I love to use my wits and figure out how I am going to meet my basic needs. Where am I going to get water and food? Where am I going to sleep? How am I going to converse with the locals? How am I going to get from Point A to Point B?

When I learn a sentence in the native language and the locals understand me, it gives me so much satisfaction that I beam with accomplishment. Often, we Americans do not need to use basic survival instincts in our everyday lives. Instead of learning how to be self-sufficient by growing or gathering or hunting our food, we go online, push a few buttons, and have the food delivered to our homes within a matter of minutes.

When I am not travelling, I read adventure travel narratives. My three most influential travel narratives are *Jungle: A Harrowing True Story of Survival* by Yossi Ghinsberg, *Paddle to the Amazon* by Don Starkell, and of course, *The Lost World of Quintana Roo* by Michel Peissel. These books engross me while I cook, wash the dishes, walk my dog, and dine with my family—it is perhaps rude to read at dinner, but I cannot help myself.

I read these books in one sitting. They let my imagination run wild with vivid images and details, and I know what the characters are thinking and feeling. I was most inspired and in awe by *Paddle to the Amazon.* Who is crazy and brave and tough enough to take their sons on a 12,000 mile journey in a canoe from Canada to the Amazon River? The author, Don Starkell, pointed out it was the adventure of a lifetime. I contacted Starkell and invited him to do slide shows, which the UMaine Bound Outdoor Office sponsored at the University of Maine. He accepted, and we connected through our mutual love for adventure. He invited me to canoe in Winnipeg with him.

Since he was an international best-selling author, I could not decline this invitation. The first night I arrived, I poured through scrapbooks of his Paddle to the Amazon trip. I learned about a second set of scrapbooks that had been put together for his Paddle to the Arctic adventure, and he gave me a sample of the Arctic beach sand. This is the trip where he lost his fingertips due to frostbite.

At the time, Starkell had almost a million dollars in the bank, but he was frugal and ate simply. During my visit, we ate lasagna dinners, raw cabbage, fish that we caught while canoeing, boxed macaroni and cheese, and bologna. The bologna we ate first while camping, and since the edges were starting to turn green, he told me to rip off that part and eat the rest. I did, and I never became ill. While camping in the wilds of the Winnipeg woods, and around the remote Gundy and Tannis Lakes, a ferocious storm blew the canoe against boulders and left a long crack in the boat. I learned from Starkell how to repair it temporarily with a special sap from the trees. My heart pounded all the way back to civilization.

For years after this adventure with Starkell, I dreamed of canoeing to the Amazon River. But then life happened, and my desire of participating in some awe-inspiring adventure dwindled until I found *The Lost World of Quintana Roo*. It is about a French native, Michel Peissel, who walked the Mexican Caribbean coastline in 1958. Between that book and the thirst for adventure that runs in my blood, the seeds of my story were sown. I was 42 years old, and my father was 65 when we crossed the Central American border by way of Cancún on foot.

Before I bring you on a journey along the Mayan coast to Central America, let me tell you about myself and my father, and some of the crazy adventures that I had as a child:

My adventures started as a kid in Raymond, Maine near Sebago Lake. Raymond is about two hours northwest of Boston. My exploratory nature comes from my parents. As a kid, I went everywhere with my dad, Richard Bailey. We skied, hiked, sledded, camped, and canoed throughout the Allagash. As a toddler and until I was a teenager, my father took me trudging in the snow to cut down our Christmas tree each year. Though sometimes, when I was very young and got too tired, my dad had to pull me through the deep snow on a sled while I eagerly carried the Christmas tree.

My dad always has a can-do attitude, never raises his voice, and he is practical and thoughtful. One of my favorite pastimes in the winter was ice skating on a pond in a sand pit behind our house. We would cook hotdogs over a small fire and drink hot cocoa. I remember ice skating on a frozen beaver stream near my house. My father had cut the branches to clear a path on the ice that seemed to weave forever through the woods. For hours, I played on the fir and pine trees cut down near my house, jumping up and down on the trampoline branches or seeing how far I could walk without falling through. These adventures made my childhood magical.

Once I became a young adult and started to live on my own, I joined the United States Navy for seven years, looking for more adventures as well as to fulfill my love for the ocean. I worked with Navy Divers in the Chesapeake Bay in Maryland, and I was responsible for driving and maintaining the diving boats. After my military duty and honorable discharge, I attended college. I returned home to study at the University of Maine. With the support of my family and with great pride, I became the first member of our family to receive a college degree, a BSc in Microbiology.

While attending University of Maine, my father and I picked up our explorations and adventures right from where we left off when I was a child. I remember an outing with my dad in Baxter State Park in February of 1993. It was a cold 22 mile cross-country skiing trip to an 1800s log cabin that was hidden away in the woods. There were no cars, no roads, and no towns. The wind chill factor was -70° F. It was so cold at night in the cabin, even with the woodstove roaring, that there was still ice on our boots the next morning; they had been sitting next to the hot stove all night! We slept intermittently with our outdoor clothes on, wearing our hats, mittens, long underwear, sweatshirts, two pair of wool socks, and jackets. We could see the outside world through the cracks of the cabin, and the wind was so strong that it kept blowing the door open in the middle of the night. I still remember wondering if I was going to wake up with frostbite. I was so fearful that I might freeze to death while I slept that I asked my dad if I could sleep with him.

He laughed and said, "No, I assure you, you won't freeze to death."

These adventures are shared only by me and my father. Ever since she experienced an off-the-beaten-path expedition with my father when she was seven, my younger sister would not join our adventures. Her last expedition featured a canoe sinking, bats flying around her head, twelve miles of wading through a lake, and hitchhiking via a logging truck. Needless to say, that experience made her even less eager to go on an adventure with Dad, especially an international expedition that would include an even greater level of danger and unknowns. In contrast to me and my father, you can find my sister relaxing at the lavish swimming pools in Cancún with a cool daiquiri in hand.

Because of these experiences of a lifetime, it was no surprise to anyone in our family when I suggested that my dad and I should follow the same path on foot that Peissel took in 1958, walking from Cancún to Belize. The year was 2005, and I was about to become in love with Mexico; I would want to explore the Yucatán like no other tourist has explored it before. The journey took seven years, and we hiked a total of 600 miles to cross the Belize border like Peissel.

While walking across miles of beautiful Mexican beaches sounds romantic, travelers should consider the following obstacles: hurricanes, difficult terrain that includes deep sand and coral and limestone boulders, numerous inlets of swamps and mangroves to cross; ferocious dogs and aggressive jungle animals, along with biting and nasty bugs; mysterious indigenous populations, language barriers, drug lords who masquerade as Mexican police and military, banditos, and squatters; less than stellar food, the omnipresent threat of heatstroke, a lack of fresh water, Montezuma's revenge, and the constant need to carry everything on your back.

Not only will you have to speak Spanish, but there is a good chance that the indigenous human population who sacrificed humans by rolling their heads down the temple stairs, according to the movie *Apocalypto* directed by Mel Gibson, only understands Mayan. The mansions of powerful drug lords may lie in the shadows along the coastline, and the inhabitants may be waiting to enslave a pair of unwitting tourists in the cocaine, heroin and meth industry. Because Mexican police are not always honest, travelers may need to resort to bribery to cross various checkpoints along the coast.

Every year, three to five tourists are eaten or mauled by crocodiles, and there are twelve species of poisonous snakes found in the Yucatán. The deadly Fer-de-Lance viper has an irritable disposition and is feared because its habitat is in close proximity to the habitats of humans. This viper camouflages effortlessly in its territory. The haemotoxin venom that seeps from its bite will cause a wound to ooze and swell, resulting in profuse internal bleeding and agonizing tissue damage. The tissue damage can be so gruesome that the ravenous bacteria will expose the bones of a victim, and a skin graft will be needed. In untreated cases, necrosis will occur, leading to gangrene and finally to amputation of a bitten limb.

Snakes are one of my favorite animals, but I would run the other way if I saw a Fer-de-Lance viper.

There is an inexhaustible list of dangerous insects in the Yucatán, but some of the most worrisome ones are the African killer bees, tarantulas, scorpions, monster grasshoppers, and colonies of termites who can squeeze almost fifty thousand residents into their homes.

Although my father agreed that walking from Cancún to Belize was a great idea, the reception of our plans was best expressed by the local who gave us a ride from our hotel and dropped us off at our starting point on the beach.

While shaking his head as he watched us walk away, the driver muttered, "*Loco gringos.*"

CHAPTER 2

How the 600 Mile Adventure Began: *Esto Es Demasiado*

• • •

My dad and I never forgot the expression of the local who thought that we were crazy to walk back to our hotel. I was certain that the local had never encountered a pair of Americans who not only ventured off the property of a five star hotel, but who also wanted to walk 20 miles into an unknown territory. We always joked that, as we continued on to Belize, the taxi driver had appropriately called us "loco gringos" right from the start of our journey.

In September of 2005, my parents asked me if I wanted to go to Mexico with them. We would be going with ten other 50 to 60 year old friends of theirs. My sister Karen would be going with her husband. We planned to stay at an all-inclusive resort in the Mayan Riviera, about 15 miles south of Cancún, located on the Yucatán peninsula, which projects like a thumb from the Gulf of Mexico. Knowing that I am not a tourist who likes sitting near the luxurious pools with a bottomless daiquiri glass, I hesitated. The trip was scheduled during the height of the hurricane season, however, and that made the trip sound exciting, so I agreed to go.

This was one of the best decisions of my life.

When I leave Maine to fly to Mexico, it is usually in late autumn or early spring. During those seasons, the trees in Maine are leafless, no flowers are in bloom, and if muddy snow is not splayed across the ground, you can see the browned grass beneath a morning frost. For six months of the year, Maine has a dull palette of green, brown, and white. Even most of the houses in Maine are painted in a similar fashion. I am surrounded by a "blah" landscape with no splashes of bright colors.

However, as I flew over Cancún for the first time, I saw the most beautiful landscape that I have ever beheld.

From the window of my plane, I stared down at the turquoise Caribbean Sea, and my heart pounded with anticipation. After ten hours of travelling, I arrived at our final destination of Iberostar Lindo in the Mayan Riviera, and I had a terrible headache. I walked onto the Caribbean beach where I saw the vibrant colors of Mexico and felt like Dorothy when the tornado whisks away the black and white set, which transforms into the colorful Land of Oz. The Mexican landscape opened up with all of the hues and shades of the rainbow: the blue and green colors of the ocean, the pink coral, the orange stucco buildings, the flowers that were shaped like orchids and tinted red, and the butterflies whose yellow and purple wings permitted them to flutter through the Yucatán jungle.

Back at the resort property with my family, I was delighted to see vibrant floral gardens, the bright and cheerful uniforms of the staff, as well as the hot peppers and bright tropical fruit that beckoned my taste buds. I was spellbound by the colorful, inviting cotton woven hammocks that had looked like the colors that pour right out of a Skittles package. The tropical sun felt heavenly on my pale skin. The sensation of that warm, powdery sand between my toes, which were tender from wearing boots all winter, was delightful.

I had suddenly forgotten about my headache!

For the next several days, I would be getting to know, and love, Mexico.

My dad and I joined the tourists in popular resort activities such as the All-Terrain Vehicle jungle tour, the resort shows, floating along in the lazy river pool, snorkeling and kayaking off the beach, and drinking the typical Coco Locos and Banana Daiquiris. When I went to the ecological, cultural, and archaeological park XCaret, I had surrendered to the magic and mystery of Mexico.

Swept off my feet, I felt as if I were twirling around in a cantina with lights dancing overhead, my body coming alive to the beat of the romantic

Latin music that the Mariachi guitarist strummed. Mexico crept in my soul. I was lured in by its promises of adventure, exotic jungles, salsa music, spicy foods, the crashing waves that came in from the Caribbean islands, and the beautiful tanned locals. The smell of the mangrove swamps, the bus stations with vehicles that waited to carry me to my destinations in other towns, and the small tortilla factories enticed me. I longed to hear the pueblo sounds of squawking roosters, the barks of dogs, waves crashing in predictable unison, the chirping of birds, and the church bells that rang in the center plazas.

My protective shell and the quietness that I had developed in Maine had disappeared, and I became uninhibited.

Most of the Maine public has heard of Cancún, which is the Mayan word for "snake nest." Some Mainers have even heard of the Yucatán and know where it is. But almost none of them know that Cancún is located in Quintana Roo and that Mexico is divided into a Federal District and 31 states; Quintana Roo is one of the 31 states. Mexico is also part of North America, not Central or South America, and is home to thousands of ruins from Mayan, Aztec and other ancient civilizations. Many of these sites have not been discovered, and there may be almost seven thousand cenotes, or sinkholes, that can be found throughout the Yucatán peninsula. Cenotes were used by the Mayans for fresh water and ceremonial purposes, specifically for sacrificing humans to their rain god. I found a few of these cenotes, some in the middle of the jungle, and was fascinated by them.

Also, let us not forget the ancient recipes of Quintana Roo, known throughout the world for foods such as tamales, mole sauce, tacos, guacamole, and tortillas. Many of these recipes incorporate chocolate, tomatoes, and corn into their dishes, and these are only three examples of crops that are native to Mexico. In the small towns, you will find señoras who teach Spanish and the preparation of authentic Mexican food to tourists with an adventurous spirit. Descendants in Mayan villages still practice beliefs and customs from thousands of years ago. Even the dress and the multicolored blouses (called huipil) of the Mayan women are still worn today. Their white dresses with colorful embroidery always appear to be clean.

I had a special opportunity to learn some little-known facts about Mexico from a native Mexican, Felipe Lupera Frutos, who is a chemical engineer at Comisión Reguladora de Energía. He told me, "When one starts to explore Mexico, very dazzling things are discovered. Many of these things can be found more easily in small pueblos than in big cities. In small pueblos ancient costumes, tools and materials are still very alive. In small pueblos, there are children playing with rudimentary toys made of wood like "baleros" and many other simple and very cheap toys. They are poor people, but you can discover part of the ancient customs. To be in touch with these people allows you to know more about the real roots of Mexico. In most of Mexico, there are still many of these small pueblos."

My opinion is that they are not "poor," but just live simply. Instead of video games, or two or three televisions and cell phones, and toys that are never opened and played with, children from these Mexican pueblos use their imaginations and play with simple toys.

In continuing with my love for knowledge of the culture in Mexico, I learned that XCaret is a Mayan archaeological site within an ecological park. For a thousand years, the inlet of XCaret was an important navigation port, ceremonial site, and a trading center for the Mayans. This was my first visit to an ecological park as well as my first cultural and natural adventure in Mexico. I felt something different, that I haven't felt when I have visited other theme and amusement parks, which mostly consist of tar, concrete, and man-made structures and giant walking mice; the park at Disney World comes to mind.

I remember walking in my bare feet across a thick rope, which had been strung across an inlet in XCaret. The body of water beneath me was not a domestic pool or a man-made swimming hole. It came from the ocean, and any creatures could be in the water waiting for me to fall; I worried about the razor teeth of crocodiles or the lash of a Portuguese Man-O-War. The ancient reptiles prowl just below the surface of the water, their mouths open, waiting for food and can attack small children, dogs, or tourists.

However, because it was a tourist park, it was well-monitored and anyone in reasonable shape could walk across the rope. While it might be scary to walk on a 3-inch diameter rope across an ocean inlet within the structured park with employees present to come running if you call for help, it was even scarier walking upon the same situation outside of the park in the wilds of the Yucatán jungle.

I also swam in the underground rivers and caves, floating from the jungle and finishing at the thick mangrove tunnels, which opened into Caribbean Sea. These small, but real adventures made me want more of Mexico on a larger scale, away from the tourists. I thought, "If these challenging adventures were inside this ecological park, what kind of adventures full of adrenalin were waiting for me out in the *real* Mexico?"

In this park, I sat alone with my father on the coral rocks near the edge of the seawater, mulling over what adventures I could undertake. My mind worked overtime as I sat in dreamy repose. My father did not yet know of the adventures for which I yearned.

The professional Mayan cultural shows that I attended with my parents at the Tlachco Auditorium in XCaret were spectacular. The performances featured warriors, kings, and a Pok-ta-pok ball game, which is best described as a mix of basketball and soccer. It is at least 3,600 years old and is played on a grassy ball court. Two teams compete to hit a 10-pound solid rubber ball (made from the rubber tree found in the rainforest) through a ring hanging on the wall of the court. The players wear protective clothing, such as knee and elbow pads, a helmet, and a wooden or leather yoke around their waists. The protective clothing is used to hit the ball with all parts of their body, except for their hands or feet.

Thousands of years ago, the victors were celebrated at a feast, and were rewarded with jewels and clothing. The unfortunate losers were decapitated, their heads, wrapped up in rubber like the game ball, and were rolled down the pyramid steps! However, some theorists suggest that the winners were sacrificed instead of the losers as a way of showing their spiritual devotion to their Gods.

The theatrical performances at XCaret gave me a brief insight into the history of Mexico. I also ate my first real tamale and churros during these shows. The tamale was one dollar; my parents, who are not ethnic eaters, purchased a cheeseburger for seven dollars. I noticed the park employees, who are native Mexicans, also ate the tamales, and I did exactly what they did: squirted lime juice on my tamale and added picante salsa. Tamales are little bundles of corn dough, filled with meat or fruit that are wrapped and steamed in banana leaves or corn husks. They are now my favorite Mexican food, and I will go to any pueblo to get one. I have never found tamales in the big tourist towns, only in the small pueblos; perhaps they are only found there because tamales are a tasty staple.

One afternoon during our stay at the Mayan Riviera resort after we experienced XCaret, my real adventures started thanks to my dad. And, I did not even have to tell him about my desires; it was like he had read my mind. My dad and I took a long walk on the beach. We walked southward over pink coral rock and limestone, and we saw blue land crabs, large marine iguanas, and brown pelicans that dove for fish. After walking for an hour, ominous thunderhead clouds darkened the sky, and it appeared we might get hit with a lightning storm while exposed on the beach.

Along this coast, there are many abandoned structures we could take shelter in if the storm got severe.

However, the storm remained off in the distance, and we decided to explore one of these vacant structures, a hotel damaged by Hurricane Emily only two or three months before our arrival. As we approached, many lizards scampered into hiding. They had taken over the stucco, concrete building, and this was their home now. The smell of their urine reeked as we walked through the iguana-infested hotel to explore all of the rooms, half expecting a skeleton to fall out of a closet. Items such as dishes and decorations were still in place, as if all of the inhabitants had gotten up and ran from the devastating hurricane that swirled upon them.

The hotel had a ghastly aura. We searched for gold coins like pirates, but instead of gold, we found a stash of authentic wooden toys and woven Mexican handmade bags. The red, blue and yellow toys looked like an old fashioned top that you pull with a string to make it spin. The colorful bags were woven of straw. I was excited to find the toys and bags because it reminded me of the colorful natives, culture, and the land that I had come to love. I wanted to take a little bit of a souvenir back with me to remember the hotel.

On the way back, we cooled off in the Caribbean Sea and rested under deserted thatched huts that were once part of popular hotels that have since been destroyed.

At the resort, after our two or three hour excursion, I took a siesta in a hammock on the beach. As I sipped a Coco Loco, I wondered what other adventures waited for me along this coastline. Mexico had fulfilled the dreams that I had as a kid about being a pirate in a tropical setting. I wanted more. I wanted to immerse myself in the culture and make friends with the people of Mexico. I wanted to explore and visit every small coastal town in Quintana Roo, to stop and chat and laugh with the locals, to practice the Spanish that I had learned in high school twenty years ago, and to have a beer or tequila. After hiking 20 miles under the tropical sun, I longed to rest under every abandoned hut along the coast, and to look out at the Caribbean Sea and watch the storms come in over the horizon, letting time pass as it only passes in Mexico.

I knew that I would not find the real Mexico near Cancún at an all-inclusive resort.

In Cancún I have been to a Pirate Island Show and Dinner, and had walked by Hooters, Coco Bongo, and Daddy O's nightclub. If you are looking for a place to party with groups of people in a noisy bar or at a disco, to drink alcohol all day while sitting in a poolside chair, to attend organized group tours on a tourist bus, to stay at a fancy hotel most likely owned by international CEOs, or to eat at expensive restaurants that serve Americanized food, then Cancún is the place for you.

I much prefer the Mexican pueblos that are rich in culture.

My sentiments are exactly what the sign says in Spanish: Esto Es Demasiado, which translates into THIS IS TOO MUCH. This neon sign, which is billboard size, is posted on the street of the Hotel Zone when you walk into Cancún. On the other side of this sign, also neon, it says: TOO MUCKING FUCH.

The idea of walking the entire coastline of the Yucatán from Cancún to Belize, with everything that my father and I needed on our backs, had not been formed yet, but I never joined the tourists on the tour buses again. I intended to see and explore Quintana Roo like no other tourist has before, without a guide. As my father and I left the resort that year, we talked about getting a job as gardeners at the resort and missing our flight. I devised seventeen jobs that I could acquire while living in Mexico to pay for my expenses in a one room cabana that would be complete with mosquito netting over the swaying hammock. I pondered an array of scenarios that would keep me in my newfound beloved land.

CHAPTER 3

South of Cancún to Playa del Carmen: Hurricanes, Pirates and Cenotes

• • •

THE WALK ALONG THE TROPICAL beach was not the only aspect of this journey that excited me; I was also thrilled by the images of pirates, treasure, and conquering physically challenging obstacles. My father had read my mind. On the last day of my first trip to Mexico in 2005, he asked me if I wanted to go on a beach excursion for an entire day. He planned to hire a taxi to take us 12 miles down Highway 307, south of XCaret, and drop us off so that we could walk back along the beach to Iberostar with a day pack that consisted of sunscreen, a camera, one bottle of water each and flip flops.

I asked, "When do we start walking?"

Highway 307 is the only major road in Quintana Roo. Twelve miles of highway could equal 30 miles of coastline. We did not anticipate how many points, inlets, and small peninsulas we would have to go around during our trek back to Iberostar.

Similarly, the highway distance of coastal Maine is 280 miles, but there are 3,500 miles of actual coastline. My father expressed concerns of two possible obstacles: How are we going get access to the beach from the highway? The public beach access proved to be a major obstacle all along this coastline. Also, are there any major rivers?

To answer these questions, we went to the attractive employees of the Iberostar Resort. They wore crisp yellow and purple uniforms, and they appreciated their customers and showed pride in sharing their lovely tropical beaches with us. The employees confirmed, "No, there are no rivers along this route." However, the staff at the resort did not know how we were going to obtain beach access. They explained that there is a law in Mexico such that all beach is public, but 20 meters from high tide, it is private property. Since most of the property in the Mayan Riviera is owned by resorts and hotels, there is no public beach access along this part of the coastline. The hotel employee telephoned one of his friends, a local boy. He gave the employee the name of the owner of Playa Los Pinos who might give us permission to cross his property for beach access. Playa Los Pinos is a property on the outskirts of Playa Del Carmen, which is a tourist town that is similar to Cancún, and XCaret.

This is where the taxi driver had dropped us off while shaking his head and muttering, "Loco gringos."

This is also where we started walking back to Iberostar.

Later on, after we were done staying at the resort and continued onto Belize, we had to figure out how to get beach access on our own, either by sneaking onto private property or walking through the swamps until we found a dirt road that lead to the highway.

Without a topographical map and with only our packs to see us through the journey, we started our adventure early in the morning. After two or three hours of walking on fine sand, we came face to face with three rivers, now known as Tres Rios Eco Park, which was not open during this time. The landscape changed from sandy beach to mangroves and jungle, with rivers running perpendicular to the ocean. It is the only one of two areas on the Yucatán peninsula that contains natural rivers. They are different than the massive rivers in Maine because they are not very wide or long. The first river was a shallow stream that we could walk across. The second river was narrow, over six feet deep, and the current ran fast.

I thought there might be crocodiles quietly lurking in the bushy mangrove, and that made me apprehensive about getting attacked or carried out to sea.

So, I hung onto a boat that was tied to a tree in the river, hoping to reach the other side as long as the rope stretched to the opposite shore. My father was eager to test out his skills on getting across, so he had already entered the water and was on his way.

However, as soon as I put my hands on the boat, a scrawny and wiry brown-skinned boy, who reminded me of Mowgli in the *Jungle Book*, came running out and yelled at me in Spanish to get away. The teenager spoke no English, and he was speaking so quickly that I did not understand a word of his Spanish. It probably did not help that he was speaking in street slang. At the time, I knew only a few words of basic Spanish.

In the meantime, my father swam with one arm rowing across the fast-moving river, while the other hand held the backpack over his head. Since the bank on the other side of the river was only eight feet wide, I was sure that my dad could do it. I, on the other hand, was still in training by my father on this adventure far away from Maine.

I was inexperienced in a third world country, and I was scared and embarrassed that this boy was going to get his father and tell him that I was stealing his boat. In a panic, I tried to relay my dilemma to the Mexican boy. I pointed to the river, and acted out "too deep, over my head." He showed me that, around the point towards the beach and away from the jungle, the river is only up to my waist. So, I started to cross the river.

As my father and I were crossing, my father lost his flip flop in the current.

Continuing to walk would be difficult because of the coral and rocks that dot this coastline. But I knew my father would find a way, perhaps wearing a dirty shoe washed up on shore or with a palm leaf tied around his foot. Luckily, his flip flop was waiting for him on the opposite side of the river, around the mangroves, on the beach. We were beaming at our good fortune to find the flip flop, and it indicated our good luck on the rest of this expedition in a third world country. Before we continued walking, my father yelled out to the boy, "*Adiós, amigo!*"

But just as quickly as the Mowgli boy with bare feet appeared, he had vanished without a trace.

Soon, we came upon mangroves and then a river with a ledge that dropped down to a bottomless ocean. This third river crossing gave us an even higher adrenaline rush. This area was wild and remote, without a hint of civilization. The only way to cross was to perform a balancing act on a large log and a rope that was strung waist high to hang onto and pray that one of us did not fall in the sea. The log was partially submerged in the seawater, and this meant that there was algae growing on it, so the log would be slippery. I was certain that there would be sea snakes and sharks and other creatures hiding beneath the cavernous ledge in the water. If one of us fell off and hit our head, or were attacked, there would be no one to save us. Even if we had a cell phone, it probably would not have worked; but my father would never hear of turning back.

Dad went across first, successfully, and then I followed.

But my heart pumped with fear. As I balanced across the log, I realized that I was over halfway to the other side, and that relieved my fears since I was closer to safety: my dad. We made it across with no incidents, again with good fortune on our side while walking our first miles on this beautiful, but still dangerous, coastline.

The three-river crossing at Tres Rio Eco Park was only the first example of inccorect information that had been relayed to us by locals. The employees at Iberostar, who live in Quintana Roo, apparently did not know about the three rivers. Whether or not they did not know because they take a bus along the highway and do not walk on the beach, I do not know.

One of the things I love about walking along this coastline is the odd structures and artful forms that nature has left, sort of like sculptures. You will find most of these pictures on the front cover of my book. We found two odd palm tree trunks with roots sticking up two feet in the surf. These roots had been washed almost smooth from the continuous waves and sand. There were lines on the trunks to make them look like the rough skin of small dinosaurs. The roots looked like arms and feet. The tree trunks were rooted in the sand and are probably still there today. We always found something like this along the coast and used our imaginations to pretend it was something else. It was like searching for and finding treasure.

While walking, we observed a large brown moth with a wing span of at least seven inches taking refuge from the ocean spray and breeze on a post under a palapa. Many pelicans perched on the rotten posts, standing in the shallow water on the lookout for their suppers before they took off and dove into the sea. I had never seen pelicans before, only seagulls in

Maine that are scavengers and seem to not work as hard to catch their dinners.

As we were walking peacefully along the beach, minding our business, three growling dogs came running at us. They were unpredictable and ready to attack us for walking into their territory. I am a dog lover, but when scruffy dogs without collars and leashes come growling like a wolf pack at me, I tremble and become ready to fight. We were without weapons since we were staying at a five-star resort and only on a day hike, so the only way to get rid of them was to swim up to our waist in the ocean. I learned that Mexico does not have a leash law. It was our first of many experiences with angry dogs.

Later on, when I had my backpack equipped for eight days, I felt better prepared to meet these seemingly aggressive dogs with my machete.

I had now been on my first real adventure outside of the tourists parks. We were misled by the hotel staff when we asked about rivers, I was suddenly caught by a Mexican teenager who thought I was stealing the boat of his father, I was chased by mangy growling mutts, and I had walked across a deep fjord on a fallen tree with only a ½ inch rope to hold onto while crocodiles, sharks, and sea snakes waited for me to fall. And I could not wait for my next adventures. I was ready to keeping walking. It was just another example of how I wanted more adventures along this exciting coastline, away from the plush resorts.

Although most of this area has resorts along the beach, some parts were still remote, with no civilization or people. We were surprised when we came upon two shacks, one with a thatched roof, in the middle of nowhere. When we discovered military camouflage shirts and pants hanging on the clothesline, we did not approach the structures, because we heard that Mexican police and soldiers are not so friendly, and some of them are not so honest. This was the first of many military posts.

I was very excited when we passed by a hotel and looked through the open window of the small rustic dining area. There were blue placemats set on the wooden table with blue tiles in the center, and the placements had the name of the hotel: Posada Capitán Lafitte. The picture of Lafitte on the placemat had the typical eye-patched pirate with a long black mustache, and the pirate hat had an emblem of the skull and cross bones.

I had just returned from New Orleans in the summer where I had explored the bayous with my mother. This is where I had first learned about the pirate Jean Lafitte. He was a privateer during the War of 1812 for the United States and was once considered a hero. When the British asked Lafitte for help in the War of 1812 and at the Battle of New Orleans, he passed on secret information to the United States. His legacy is still a mystery, as mysterious as the Louisiana bayous, where some of his gold doubloons from captured merchant ships are hidden.

One legend is that his body and his treasures are buried somewhere on the Yucatán peninsula. Some believe that a snake that is as big as a dragon with razor fangs appears if anyone gets too close to the treasure. Another story tells of a skeleton holding a sword that is rusty and studded with jewels, standing guard over the gold of Lafitte.

It is interesting to note that in *Incidents of Travel in Yucatán* the author, John L. Stephen, mentioned crossing paths with one of Lafitte's prisoners on Isla de Mujeres, which is off the coast of Cancún and is part of Quintana Roo. The loyal prisoner, who appeared to not be entirely held captive against his will, talked about Lafitte dying in his arms. Perhaps the prisoner became fond of Lafitte while in captivity and promised to watch over his loot to the bittersweet end. This is one notable reference that Lafitte possibly died in the Yucatán.

After passing the Posada Capitán Lafitte and filling my head with pirates and what it was like living in those days, I was startled when I realized that we were approaching our resort back in the present. I thought, "This seven hour adventure was even better than XCaret or the mini beach walk." My dad always wanted to know what was around the next bend, so I knew he was thinking the same thing. However, this hike was like a stroll on the beach for us compared to the rest of the strenuous 580 miles that we would decide to attempt on foot with "our house on our backs," to Central America.

This day was a perfect ending to my first visit to Mexico, and I knew I needed to return.

After leaving Mexico that year, for the entire winter I read all that I could find about the country, particularly Quintana Roo and off-the-beaten-path guides and cultural books. I found all sorts of non-touristy excursions that we could participate in, such as Goyo Adventures at a Mayan Sweat Lodge and Ranch, renting a Jeep and driving to small fishing villages, and swimming in magical sinkholes. My newfound love of the Mexican Caribbean and the small coastal pueblos brought me and my parents back in May of 2006.

We stayed at Iberostar again. We rented a Jeep to explore deep in the Yucatán jungle and visited a remote cenote and a Mayan ranch out of Puerto Morelos. Some of these roads we travelled were Mayan sacbeob roads. The Mayans built sacbeob roads thousands of years ago out of limestone and coral, which made them white. The Mayans walked on these roads in the jungle, and because the roads were white, it made it easy for them to see during the night, especially in the moonlight.

One of the most natural and mysterious wonders of the Yucatán peninsula is the cenotes. I find them captivating because they are very peaceful and I know they were used for sacrifices. The Yucatán land is porous and made of limestone. Therefore, all of the major rivers are underground, some with majestic cave systems. There are thousands of cenotes on this peninsula. Most of them are undiscovered, unique, and a lot of them are in remote inland areas. One cannot know where all the cenotes are in the Yucatán.

Cenotes have fresh, cool water that is as clear as crystal; it is great for swimming and serves as drinking wells for the people of the Yucatán. I have even been to a man-made local swimming pool made for the people of the pueblo where the source of water to fill the pool is from a cenote. They are also refreshing for snakes and other creatures that like to hide in the crevices of the walls of cenotes. They can be entirely underground, partially underground, on the surface like a lake, or with open walls. Cenotes are mystical and considered sacred. Mayans sacrificed their bodies to the

Rain God by throwing themselves into the cenote in times of drought. At Chichén Itzá, Mayans threw themselves into the dark waters of the Well of Sacrifice 70 feet below. In 1904, the archaeologist Edward Herbert Thompson drained the sacred cenote and found human skeletons of children and adults, jade, gold discs, Mayan god figures, vases, and obsidian knives.

Even though Puerto Morelos is near Cancún, it is still a small and quaint sleepy fishing town that is visited by some tourists. However, these tourists are looking to immerse themselves in the native culture. Puerto Morelos has all of the quirks that someone could want: a fishing dock and a lighthouse, a jungle and farmer's markets, small hotels, an internet café, the former Mama's Bakery where the owner was the first person who suggested that I should write a book on the adventures that I have undertaken with my dad, several restaurants, a park, tiendas, and a variety of shops, including an English bookstore. The lighthouse is a symbol of the town because it was damaged by a hurricane in 1967 and still leans heavily in the sand. Puerto Morelos is one of my favorite pueblos along this coast. One could find tamales here at El Tios.

My father and I resumed our beach hiking from the previous year, but this time, we travelled 15 miles north on Highway 307. We were dropped off on the highway north of Puerto Morelos, outside of Cancún, and our first obstacle was a Federal Zone concrete compound. The 10 foot tall gates, fences, and security personnel prevented us from continuing our walk on the beach. To find the beach again, we had to go back into town and go around the complex. I was sure that security personnel, armed with their high-powered guns, were watching us.

We noticed that the beach in this area, from Puerto Morelos to Iberostar, was not as pretty as the stretch from the Mayan Riviera. This beach was comprised mostly of mangroves and seagrass, which made the beach look dirty and reek like rotten vegetation. The water was brown, and we had to walk in deep seagrass that lined the coastline. Perhaps this was due to the wrath of Hurricane Wilma, which hit the Yucatán in October 2005, seven months before my parents and I returned to the area.

According to internet reports and NOAA, it was the strongest hurricane ever recorded in the Atlantic basin, stalling for five days over Cancún and the island of Cozumel, with five feet of rain and wind speeds of 185 mph. Hurricane Wilma wiped out all of the palm trees in Puerto Morelos.

When we arrived, there were only replanted baby palms along the beach. All of the live vegetation on the mangroves was completely drowned and dead.

When I flew into Cancún that year, there were huge patches of brown because there were no leaves on the mangroves. I have *before* (Sept 2005) and *after* (May 2006) pictures from Wilma in the same spot on the beach: the *before* picture shows lush green, healthy mangroves, and the *after* picture shows only brown dead vegetation with dirty seawater. We passed and explored many beach houses that Wilma destroyed. With pieces of concrete everywhere, and the floors caved in, and the furniture blown away, and broken wires and tile, and beach sand that flew inside the house covering even the toilet seat, it looked like a bomb had detonated in these beach houses. Because the Yucatán peninsula sticks out like a thumb in the path of hurricanes, it is constantly battered each year.

Michel Peissel writes about the strength of these hurricanes by examining a leaf that he saw in the West Indies: "This leaf had been so hardened by the force and pressure of the wind that when it was hurled into the door of a house it buried itself in the wood like a razor blade."

Speaking of hurricanes, one of the highlights of walking this stretch of the coast was the large ship named Quintana Roo that was beached from Wilma near Puerto Morelos. The ship was definitely out of place on the beach, and it made you wonder what happened. Maybe the water receded during the storm, leaving the ship stuck deep in the sand. Perhaps a powerful wave hurled it onto the beach at the height of a tempest. Quintana Roo looked like an abandoned ghost ship that had been sitting there, rusting away. We did not see any security guards in the area, so using an oil drum and a rope to assist us, we climbed aboard approximately fifteen to twenty feet to investigate the steel giant.

Quintana Roo was a car ferry built in the 1960s for a coastal route in Scotland, and some years later, it was sold to Mexico. Ironically, I visited New Orleans in July 2005, and after I left, Hurricane Katrina devastated the city in August 2005. Then I went to Mexico in September 2005, and after I left, Hurricane Wilma ravaged the Yucatán. My parents called me a "jinx."

I enjoyed my exploration of the beached ship, but my father wanted to keep walking. So, we continued on.

Imagine that you are hiking step by step in soft hot sand for hours in the 100° F tropical sun, wishing that there was a store around the next bend with an ice cold bottle of water to drink. You have not seen a soul for miles. You are also getting sorely sunburned and sweaty, and your mouth is dry and scratchy, and your legs are aching. The hot bottles of water that you carry are not adequately quenching your thirst, and they leave the taste of toxic plastic in your mouth. All of a sudden, while you are walking in the middle of nowhere and look around the next point, two large yellow tents with blue words appear: "CORONA EXTRA."

Could it be a dream or a hallucination? Are you delirious from heat exhaustion?

That is exactly how we felt when we came upon these tents in the middle of the deserted beach. My dad said, "Let's check it out. There must be some reason those tents are there."

Indeed, there was a reason. Mexican employees were selling ice cold beer, Gatorade and water that were stored in coolers. They were working under these tents because there were tourists on an All-Terrain Vehicle Tour riding through the jungle to the beach, stopping here for a refreshing drink. In Spanish, I told the Mexican man in a tropical coral-colored shirt that we were hiking from Puerto Morelos to Iberostar in the Mayan Riviera. I asked if we could have a drink. He spoke with surprise and disbelief as he gave us two cold Gatorades and bottled water to replenish our supply. He did not charge us. Since this establishment dealt with tourists, the Mexicans were well-accustomed to English and spoke fluently.

We made it back at the end of the day, me with my sunburns and my dad with a twisted ankle, but we were both giddy with excitement as we told my mother about our adventures.

At this point, we have covered over 50 miles of the Yucatec Maya coastline on foot, walking from the beach south of Cancún to XCaret. It was two months later, over the summer, back in Maine, when I found and read *The Lost World of Quintana Roo.* I found an antique edition online; I really wanted it, so I paid the highest price. I also found out that the author, Michel Peissel, passed away sometime in the early 2000s, so I was not able to share notes with him on the same route that he travelled almost 50 years ago. My father was equally fascinated by the book. The summer of 2006 is when I suggested walking the rest of the way to Belize, making no reservations, sleeping only in cabañas, on the beach, or in abandoned structures, and carrying everything we needed on our backs. The two of us decided that we would hike 120 miles in 9 days every May, continuing our walk from Cancún to Belize.

CHAPTER 4

Preparations: *The Lost World of Quintana Roo*, Machete, and Maps

• • •

In preparation for this exciting adventure, I want to tell you why Peissel walked this route. I also want to explain some of the differences between 50 years ago and now. These differences affected when we would go, how we planned our water and food, what we carried in our backpacks, and how we trained all year to keep in shape for our grueling tropical hike.

In *The Lost World of Quintana Roo*, Peissel intended to discover unexplored ruins. But he also had dreams of adventure in the real tropics and was the first white man to explore this treasured coast. He graduated from Harvard and left his job as a Wall Street banker and found himself stranded on the barren, savage coast of Quintana Roo—alone. Equipped with only a suit jacket, trousers, sandals, hammock and a few other items in his henequen bag, Peissel started to walk. In 1958, this coastline was unknown to the world, and it was dangerous. Cancún was not discovered until the 1970s. Peissel encountered bandits, pirates, murderers, chicleros, Indians, and outlaws as well as venomous snakes and scorpions during his journey to British Honduras, which is now known as Belize. He mostly lived off tortillas given to him from chicleros at the chicle camps, and he also hunted turtles on the beach.

Chicle camps were once an industry where chicle sap was gathered from the sapodilla tree and processed for chewing gum; think of the brand Chiclets. The chewing gum was invented in 1858 and was once more harvested than wood because, during World War I and II, the gum was included in the rations for the soldiers at war. It was also popular in baseball card packets that were circulated in the 1930s. The chicle industry paid the chicleros, who often were members of the indigenous populations, Koreans who were sold off as slaves, or migrants. After working in this dangerous jungle with the snakes, malaria, and machete accidents, many of the workers turned to the saloons, booze, violent bar fights and sometimes murder. Peissel met these shady characters who fearlessly wielded their guns and machetes.

The white sap has not been harvested since the 1960s due to overtapping and the trees dying off, but there has been a recent interest in reviving the industry to provide an alternative to the cheaper synthetic rubber that is produced for the chewing gum that we currently use. I did not see any of these dangerous camps, but while walking in the remote jungles of the Yucatán searching for cenotes, my father and I did find the sapodilla trees with V-cuts from machetes where the sap runs down and is collected.

After reading *The Lost World of Quintana Roo* and about chicle campus along the coastline, the idea started spinning in my head: it is possible to walk the entire way to Belize since there are no major rivers in the Yucatán. I shared my thoughts with my dad that summer. We would make no reservations, sleeping only in cabañas, on the beach, or in abandoned structures, carrying everything we needed on our backs to Belize. Because of our family and work schedules, we did not walk the entire 550 miles at one time. Each year, we walked an average of 120 miles south in nine days, usually walking 15 miles a day, starting where we left off the previous year. It took us four years to complete as we only took vacation time for the trip. We always left in May because this was after spring break, which meant fewer tourists, and May also precedes the hurricane and rainy seasons. Because we did not make any reservations, it was advantageous for us not to have the hotels and cabañas full.

During the snowy Maine winters, I researched the next stretch of 120 miles that we would be hiking. Throughout the night, I poured over topographical maps of Mexico and Belize, both countries spread out on my living room floor. I measured the coastline with string and made notes on the maps to mark the mileage. It was important for me to mark towns with possible water and food replenishment at increments of 15 miles, figuring we could walk that distance in a day. I would also use sources such as the aerial Costa Maya beach photos of the LocoGringo website and books like *The Adventure Guide to the Yucatán* by Bruce and June Concord. I made notes of the landscape and possible structures where we could stay overnight.

For example, there was a town on the topographical map named XCacel, and the guidebooks raved how it was a popular place for watching sea turtles hatch from their eggs. We thought that, if the town was on the map, we should be able to replenish our water and food supplies and have some place to sleep.

However, when we arrived in what we thought was XCacel, we found two white stucco buildings abandoned in the middle of nowhere. That is what the town of XCacel consisted of—a pair of uninhabited buildings. We never did get water or food or rest, and the only two people in this town did not speak a word of English.

I knew it was important for me to brush up on my high school Spanish during the winter months in Maine. Luckily, I had done well in my classes and only had to take some online tutorials and complete workbooks at home. That was sufficient for basic conversation. However, as our hiking led us out of the tourist region and beyond Tulum into the Costa Maya remote area, more advanced formal classes were needed. My father speaks zero Spanish. Since he was almost always ahead of me, his lack of Spanish was a disadvantage, especially when looking down the barrel of a machine gun.

My dad and I would exchange information throughout the winter. I was the expedition leader and my dad was the financial advisor. Assuming that the geology of the coastline would be the same today as it was in 1958, I kept a small journal of notes from *The Lost World of Quintana Roo*, noting the landscape as Peissel described it. I would transcribe details about the rocky areas and coral, locations of various remote ruins, inlets, mangroves and swamps, and coconut plantations. I took this journal with me while hiking and compared my notes to what I actually saw.

My main concern about walking 120 miles in nine days was carrying a backpack containing everything that I would need, especially since I have acute scoliosis. Our LL Bean day packs with chest and waist belts averaged about 18 pounds, including our three 20 ounce bottles of water. We needed the backpacks and our supplies to be light enough for tropical hiking. I love my sky blue, sea-salt crusted backpack. During the last 100 miles, I suggested to my dad that we should name our packs.

He laughed and said, "I will think about the names while we hike. When the backpack is sitting beside me and I know it has everything I need, it is my friend. But when it is on my back, it is my enemy."

Dad decided to name them Old Fart and Wanna Be. His pack was Old Fart because of his age, and mine was Wanna Be because, while in Central America after crossing the border, we saw a young couple who were professional backpackers. My dad knew I wanted to be like them and continue walking through Central America. I have become so attached to my backpack that whenever I travel, I never carry a suitcase. I feel so carefree when I have everything I need on my back; I can go anywhere with it, without the burden of a bulky suitcase on wheels.

I meticulously reviewed each item that was going in the pack, confirming the necessity with my dad and comparing items. It was essential that we did not carry the same items that could be shared. I would carefully trim each topographical map section, with markings of notes that we would need that year, to eliminate unnecessary space and weight, and place them in ziplock bags. For our hydrocortisone and antibiotic creams, I would place a small pea size amount in two sterile microfuge tubes from my labs. Every ounce counted. I also wrapped a small amount of duct tape around my pencil or pen. I also wrapped some dental floss around my child-sized toothbrush. All clothing items were tightly rolled.

The remaining items in my backpack included the following:

Two pairs of shorts
One T-shirt
Two tank tops
Two pairs of underwear
One pair of socks
Two bathing suits
Sunglasses
One bra
Flip flops
Sneakers
Teva sandals
Trail mix
Ziplock bags

Machete
Digital camera
Trimmed topo maps
Toiletries
Small pad of paper for journal
Spanish travel dictionary
Candle
Army hammock
Mosquito net
Bandana
15 SPF sunscreen
30 SPF sunscreen w/ bug spray
Three 20 ounce bottles of water

Baseball hat
Credit card
Passport
400.00 USD
One pair of pants
Maine post cards
Light scarf for sun
Lip balm
Driver's license
Waist pack
Money/travel bag
Light canvas bag

The items that my father packed included the following:

Light hiking boots
One pair of socks
One T-shirt
One pair of pants
Two bathing suits
Two tank tops
Two pairs of underwear
Teva sandals
15 SPF sunscreen
Baseball hat

Toiletries
Mosquito net
Trail Mix
Bandana
Two trash bags
First aid kit
Waterproof matches
Hunter's knife
Lip balm
Three 20 ounce bottles of water

Passport
Airline tickets
Credit card and cash
1,200.00 USD
Fingernail clippers
Army hammock
Rope
Ziplock bags
Driver's license

My machete tended to be an interesting topic of conversation for kids and adults, both in Mexico and during slide shows in the United States. It has a two foot blade and fits perfectly in my backpack, protected in a canvas sheath. Of course, we did not carry our backpacks on the plane; we checked them in as luggage. And every time we went through customs and immigration at the Cancún airport, I worried about our machetes and hunting knives in our backpacks. My father and I always joked about who would get the red light and inspection.

How many tourists were carrying machetes in their bags? And why were those tourists carrying one, especially a female tourist?

We did not want to sit in a back room in Mexican customs while explaining to the officers, who may or may not speak comprehensible English, that we were walking from Cancún to Belize. I was certain that they would not believe us. I received the red light only once; the inspection officer placed her gloved hand in my backpack and must not have felt the machete because she did not even blink her eyes. I also noticed that she was distracted by a conversation with her coworker.

If an inspector wanted to be difficult and take away my machete, would we have to cancel the hike for that year? Not a chance—we could probably just buy or trade one from a local on the streets. But I did not want to get into an argument with a Mexican inspector. My machete was essential for opening wild coconuts to keep us hydrated, and when necessary, it could be used for protection against jungle animals or bandits, especially when sleeping on the beach.

I have also been known to take an old light jacket with me to the airport in Portland, Maine before our departure because it is cold in May. Right before I get on the plane, I discard or give away the jacket because I cannot carry it in my backpack. On this trip, there was a more important reason that I needed to take this jacket: instead of taking a taxi to the Portland airport from Maine Mall Motors where my dad left his car, he wanted to walk to the airport, which was 45 minutes away, at 3:30 am!

But I did not mind because it provided us with a preview of the next nine days.

In addition to our research and packing, we had to condition our old bodies throughout the year to prepare for the physically challenging portion of the 550 mile hike. Often, we walked in the sand and on the coral in the 110° F temperatures. The sand was not always hard packed. Sometimes, we walked through four to six inch deep soft sand, which added resistance and made our trek more arduous, adding pounds to our backpack. The Yucatán coastal terrain consists of 60% limestone rock or coral, and only 40% silky white sand. I calculated that we were going to expend 3,000 to 4,000 calories hiking seven to eight hours in one day.

I usually lost about 10 pounds during these hikes.

Since we have prioritized exercise throughout our lives, the training for me and my father came easy. Seeing how much the human body can endure under extreme conditions appeals to me. During the five winter months in Maine, I participated in Zumba, aerobic classes, and cross-country skiing. During the other months, I ran on wooded trails with my Siberian husky. If the conditions were right in March, I walked in the slushy snowy trails because it simulates walking in sand. By April and May, I walked with my backpack, full weight, for practice. I kayaked, biked, played volleyball and tennis, and surfed. I have participated in a number of races to support research for curing cancer, and these events include the Komen Race for the Cure.

Completing boot camp in the Navy provided me with a mindset that is geared towards a lifetime of physical fitness!

My Dad and I constantly foster competition between us, and to make sure I gave my physical best as a kid, he always chanted to me, "Anything you can do, I can do better." To challenge me to perform better, he would say, "If you can touch the ball, you can catch it." Not only that, but my dad also had training in active duty with the US Army while stationed in Korea in 1965 and 1966. He describes my US Navy training as being "candy ass." But of course, squids are far superior to grunts. In addition, my father has played basketball all of his life, including on the National Senior Olympics team, and he has won numerous medals. He was also the number one 3-point shooter in all of New England for his age group.

In addition, he cross-country skis every weekend in the winter and plays volleyball and tennis, and surfs, and bikes. Even though my father was 65 years old when we crossed the border, the whole 550 miles, except for one day, he was way ahead of me.

With our preparations completed, May of 2007 was finally upon us. I was so excited to return to my newfound love, backpacking on the tropical beach with my dad, and seeing the real Mexico. At last, we were ready for our big journey.

CHAPTER 5

Paamul to Tulum: *The Found World of Quintana Roo* and the Raft

• • •

THE NEXT 120 MILE SECTION of our trek would be from Paamul to Tulum. During this part of our journey, we passed through the pueblos of Puerto Aventuras, Xpu Há (pronounced Ish-puha), Akumal, XCacel, and Tan'kah. South of XCaret and Playa del Carmen, Paamul is a backpacker's cabana that has beach access. Since my father had previously walked the XCaret beaches years ago, Paamul seemed like a fitting place to start.

I was so excited to continue this journey to Central America that I did not notice or concern myself with any obstacles when I conducted my winter research. However, because we only carried three to four 20 ounce bottles of water for every 15 to 20 miles with coconut water as a supplement, I noted places along the way where we could replenish our water supply. I also noted the mileage between these stops.

But when actually hiking, the distance was farther than we anticipated because of the inlets, turns, man-made obstacles, mangroves, and jungle. Since we were still in the tourist sections, there would be plenty of places to stay overnight. We never stayed in resorts while hiking.

I took note of certain landmarks from *The Lost World of Quintana Roo* in my journal:

- A small well, dug by author, three yards away from the sea for fresh water (although I doubted that I would find this well, I made a note specifically because it was possible for us to dig a well, too, if we needed fresh water).
- In Xpu Há, a marsh that neighbors three pyramids, which are 300 yards away.
- In Akumal, a temple on a large rock in the sea. After that it is nothing but rocky coast to Tulum and a lot of coconuts.

I also noted to be watchful for a very poisonous snake, the Fer-de-Lance or *cuatro narices* (four nostrils).

Upon arriving at the Cancún airport, we changed our US dollars for pesos; 400.00 USD got us about 4,000.00 pesos at the time. Many local hotels and cabanas do not accept credit cards, and sometimes they do not accept USD either; this was something that we discovered as we walked south and left the tourist zone. The people who manage those hotels and cabanas probably lack the technology to accept credit cards or exchange from American dollars to pesos, and they may want to stay true to their local traditions.

Instead of dealing with an American terminal and all of the tourist representatives, my dad and I immediately went to the Mexican terminal to look for the local bus. We noticed right away that the airport employees no longer heckled us about luggage or transportation.

Once we were out of Cancún, our plan was to stay overnight in Puerto Morelos then take a 'chicken bus' down Highway 307 to our starting point. A chicken bus is a slang term for the local Mexican buses. In smaller pueblos or the countryside, people often share a bus with chickens, goats, or other farm animals. Poor but colorful people often fill chicken buses, carrying their loads of household goods. The bus windows are usually open, blowing in humid air while driving through muddy and rutted jungle roads with crates of chickens on top.

Even though the local buses in Quintana Roo are dirt cheap, they are still comfortable. Most of them have air conditioning and small televisions with movies in Spanish. Taking the chicken bus is a great way to travel and provides opportunities to practice the language and befriend the natives. A traveler just has to know a little bit of Spanish, lack a schedule, and have a sense of adventure.

From this point forward, we traveled the way that the locals do; it was thrilling. The bus does not go right to your destination. Instead, the driver takes detours to pick up more interesting passengers. Although this lengthens the ride, the detours allow a traveler to see more of the countryside. I have ridden with many interesting locals, but a particularly memorable local comes to my mind: When I tried to tell a mother her young daughter was pretty in Spanish, I used the word *bonita*, and the mother shyly turned away and shook her head like I had used the incorrect word.

Since we never had a plan or made reservations for transportation in Mexico, we had to figure it out ourselves; we had to employ our wits for basic survival. We used ADO and MAYAB local buses throughout our journey in Quintana Roo on the highway, and we used ADO bus to get from the airport to Puerto Morelos. To go from the airport to Puerto Morelos is 4.00 USD. Using other forms of transportation costs a person 10 times as much while traveling along the Mayan Riviera.

The disadvantage with local buses is that they will always drop us off on Highway 307, and this means that we have to walk or find other transportation to the pueblo. Usually, though, we can find a collectivo.

Collectivos are like shuttle buses that locals use to get around town, and they are much smaller than the local buses. They are usually white on the outside with just a metal frame. There are sixteen hard plastic seats on the inside. I hardly ever saw tourists on collectivos, but we used one to reach the center of town in Puerto Morelos at a cost of about 40 cents.

We arrived in Puerto Morelos, and our first complication was the band of the Labrador dog hat that my father liked to wear: it broke. Instead of buying a new hat, my dad insisted on keeping the scraggly but sentimental one. While sitting on the edge of the Mexican highway near a pueblo, he pulled out his hunting knife and attempted to fix the hat by using string to hold the band together. Not surprisingly, this caused some commotion, and we received plenty of strange, and possibly concerned, stares on the streets of this small town.

Dad and I stayed overnight in Puerto Morelos at Amar Inn, a local beach hotel that was run by a family. The white stucco hotel was decorated with diving treasures, including cannons from the 1700s and antique anchors that the grandfather had collected from the reef about 200 feet away. We stayed on the top floor, and ascended as if we were climbing up a treehouse. Slabs of wood had been nailed to a palm tree, and these were the steps that spiraled up to the loft; they wobbled when we climbed them.

This hotel was memorable for us because of our breakfast. My dad loves toast for breakfast. Everywhere we went in Mexico, he always asked for toast. He never seemed to get it. In fact, the locals never understood what he wanted—I doubt that Mexicans make toast because they tend to make tortillas instead.

While there, I used my basic Spanish to speak with a pair of handsome young boys named Gabriel and Mauro who were playing board games on the steps of the hotel. They were about eight years of age, seemingly quiet and shy, but they allowed me to take their picture while proudly posing close to each other. Mauro smiled, and Gabriel stood more seriously. Their mother was the maid of the hotel, and they lived there. The word "BIMBO" was printed on Mauro's blue and yellow shirt. It did not register at the time, but when I was putting my slide show together for the public in Maine, I embarrassedly realized that the word *bimbo* in America means a floozy woman. I wondered why this young boy would have these words on his shirt, so I looked it up and discovered that *bimbo* is the name of the largest bread factory in all of Latin America, similar to Kraft and Unilever in the United States. The BIMBO Corporation sponsors most of the popular Mexican soccer team Club América.

Puerto Morelos is such an interesting town. I was delighted to see a farmer's truck pass slowly by on the dirt street with mangoes and watermelons as cargo. The farmer addressed the town through a speaker horn, announcing that his produce was for sale. I purchased a mango for five cents, and it was the juiciest and most delicious mango that I have ever eaten.

Back at the hotel, because we only brought a small amount of clothes with us in our backpacks in the tropics, it was important to me to wash my two pairs of pink underwear. Before we fell asleep for that night in our cozy and small room, I managed to wash them and hung them out to dry. In the morning, I discovered that the humid tropical air did not dry them; the humidity had made them damper! In a hurry to start hiking on the beach for the day, I tied them on my backpack so that they would dangle in the sea breeze, hopefully drying. Little did I know that I was about to be embarrassed again right after thinking *bimbo* was a floozy woman!

As we walked to the center of town in the morning to travel by MAYAB bus to Paamul, we had to take a collectivo to reach the bus station on Highway 307. When we were travelling through the small town of Pueblo Morelos on the collectivo to the bus station, the small shuttle was full of Mexican construction workers. My dad and I were still able to get on it, but we had to stand in the front with our backs to all of the workers. My dad was in the front while I stood behind him. We also had our packs on our backs. It is not unusual to be allowed to stand on a packed bus in Mexico, probably because they want to make as much money as possible. As I looked behind me at all of the faces of the workers, they were either smiling or laughing at me. I thought it was kind of odd, but quickly turned around.

Once again, the buses dropped us off on the side of the highway in the 110° F sun, in the middle of nowhere, leaving us to walk along the back roads to the beach. We obtained beach access at Paamul and started hiking for about two hours south along the coast.

As we walked, I realized something:

It was not until two hours later, as we were hiking, that I remembered my pink underwear was still hanging on my backpack while I was standing on the bus! Mexican laborers probably do not see many female tourists with underwear hanging from their backpacks on the chicken buses. My father and I laughed for a while as we continued to hike.

As we covered our first of hundreds of miles with our backpacks, I realized that not all of the Caribbean coast of Mexico is comprised of fine, powdery sand. The contrast was striking, and the coastline was difficult to walk on. Miles of flat crater rocks with crevices where creepy-crawlies hid, coral boulders, and changing patterns of pebbles, sand, and rock lined the beach from Puerto Aventuras and Tulum. It was challenging to walk this type of terrain for miles with an 18 pound backpack.

My father had no problems with the weight of his backpack or the exhausting terrain; he always walked ahead of me, excited but cautious about what lurked around the next bend.

While looking down the headlands, we realized that this peninsula was extremely long. Every time we looked over the horizon to the next point of land, we said, “Around that bend must be the next town.” But of course, it rarely turned out to be true. We usually walked the next three bends and another ten miles before we reached our destination for the day. When we asked for directions, from either tourists or locals at resorts, we never received an accurate distance because they talked about highway miles. We had to add three times the mileage when walking the coast.

We also encountered a major problem during the stretch between Paamul and Tulum. This stretch contains mostly all-inclusive resorts where guests pay one price—usually thousands of dollars—in advance for the week. Upon their arrival, the resort staff gives the guests a bracelet that they wear during their stay. This allows them to receive drinks, food, and entertainment without paying cash. At these resorts, there are beach bars that serve drinks and sometimes grilled snacks such as nachos and hamburgers. Even though we had money and credit cards, the beach bars and restaurants at these resorts did not deal with currency. Therefore, it was impossible for us to replenish our food and water during this stretch.

My dad and I walked 20 miles each day to reach the next pueblo where we could purchase food and water. We did not drink or eat at scheduled intervals. We only drank and ate when water or food was available. To keep walking, we devised ways that we could get food and water, and we had to be creative. My father hid in the beach grass or behind boulders with our backpacks while I approached the beach bars. Because I spoke some Spanish and am a female, I often sweet-talked my way into getting drinks from the Mexican bartenders who were mostly males. The natives never suspected tourists entering the property from the coast! I had to hide my wrists underneath the counter to hide the fact that I was not wearing a bracelet. There was never a time when this idea failed us. We almost never drank alcohol, opting instead for water, pineapple juice, and Cokes. After walking 15 miles, drenched with sweat, the cold Cokes satisfied us the most; it felt like we found the mother lode of all treasures.

We also rehydrated by receiving water from the tourists who were mostly Americans and Canadians. We told them that we were walking to Belize, and the friendly and shocked tourists always gave us their bottles of water. The tourists liked our tales of adventures. Perhaps it made them feel like they were taking part by helping us when we needed it.

Whether sweet-talking my way into a drink or enticing the tourists with our daring tales, we always had a way to restock our needed supplies.

Once, we snuck a cool and refreshing swim in a resort pool. My father enjoyed this stretch of the Yucatán peninsula because many of the female tourists would sunbathe topless. However, we had to be careful about entering these properties on the beach; public access was prohibited. Sometimes, the resort security yelled at us, and we kept walking until we found another resort with no security. Some of the all-inclusive resorts that we walked by included the Xpu Há Palace, El Dorado, Oasis, Bahia Principe, and Grand Sirenis.

When Peissel walked this coastline in 1958, he also hid behind boulders, but for a very different reason: he was hiding from three murderous men with machetes that knew his camera was worth money. Peissel called this land a "Lost World" because it was savage and barren. Today, this coastline is dotted with grand resorts and thousands of tourists. Because of this, I like to call it *The Found World of Quintana Roo.* This is the name of my website and fundraiser I developed to gather donations for cancer research at the Maine Institute for Human Genetics & Health. One would think that, because of all the rich resorts in this area, we would have no problem getting food or drinks. The opposite was true; we had a hard time, as Peissel did, but for very different reasons!

After walking all morning following my underwear fiasco and refreshed by our "free" Cokes and cool swim in the pool, we came to our first obstacle, the Puerto Aventuras marina. I knew this might be a problem when I did my research over the winter, but when I brought it to the attention of my father, he shrugged and said, "We will just walk around it."

But this would take us miles out of the way!

Puerto Aventuras boasts that it is a safe haven for fishing boats and yachts in the area during hurricanes like Wilma. This area looked snotty and rich, lined with condos, distinct compared to outside in the real world of Mexico on the "other side." It reminded me of yacht clubs in the United States. There was not much of a beach, only four inlets with cement docks and sidewalks. We had to wade through the water to continue or walk around the docks, all the while dreamily staring at the luxury yachts moored at the marina. When we looked down in the clear water, we spied a spotted eagle ray gracefully flapping its gigantic wings, colorful fish darting about, and large, dangerous spiny black sea urchins. Dolphins showed off their swimming and jumping skills to the tourists wandering around on the docks.

We also saw the most common coastal animals, the large marine iguanas, sunning themselves. They always just seemed to sit there, soaking up the rays without a care in the world—what a life! Since this is a public world class marina, it was a great place to stop for lunch, so we indulged. I always prefer the local cuisine, so I ordered chicken tacos with guacamole, onions, cilantro, and lots of hot sauce while my dad stuck with a cheeseburger.

Walking through the marina turned out to be like a maze with concrete paths zigzagging throughout the mangroves and jungle, and there was no apparent exit.

It was noon, the hottest part of the day. Without the cool sea breezes found on the beach and the ocean, the heat can be deadly, and so can the bugs. Not only were we getting lost, drenched with sweat and desperate with thirst, but the bugs were making us crazy by buzzing around our heads as we senselessly swatted at them. As we went around in circles, all the scenery looked the same, and I panicked. But I knew my dad would get us out of the maze eventually.

Eventually, we came to a large steel gate about 25 feet high. We discussed the possibility of this belonging to a house or maybe the mansion of a drug lord. Did we dare to stop and ask how much further before we reached the beach? It did not matter, though, because there was the pleasant sight of a blue turquoise color, probably a lagoon, on the other side of the gate. At that moment, we felt relieved and overjoyed because a lagoon meant that we were close to the ocean and to continuing our walk.

Soon, we would feel the cool breezes again and be out of this sticky jungle maze.

However, as we approached the gate and the "blue lagoon," we realized that we were delirious because the blue color was only the gate painted blue. Laughing, we backtracked and took a different path. We soon found our way out, but not without experiencing one more hallucination. Because my dad is always in front of me, he noticed something large and black run across our path in the jungle.

Concerned, I asked him, "What was it?"

He answered, "I don't know because it ran too quickly, maybe a jaguar or a man wearing dark clothes!"

I hoped it was the rare jaguar, but because were in such bad shape with heat exhaustion and thirst, we may have been starting to see things; our minds were playing tricks on us.

Feeling comfortable on the beach again, we followed the cement paths until I caught sight of a curious spectacle. I quickened my pace in excitement when I spied a small and remote Mayan ruin near a lagoon – right in front of me! Barbed wire secured the ruin. Lily pads and seaweed grew in this lagoon, and a Mayan Indian fished in this seemingly prime spot. He had a distinctly Mayan appearance. His skin was copper brown, and he had slanted eyes and a long, curved nose, and he was of a short stature. His black hair was slicked back, and he only wore shorts and flip flops. We stopped to chat and found he spoke good English. He was pleasant and educated. He told me that paintings from his ancestors were located within the ruin, created thousands of years ago. I wanted to sneak inside for a closer look, but decided against it since there was barbed wire strung tightly around the ruin.

Before exiting these sidewalks, my father and I passed by deserted orange and yellow villas. A large iguana, at least 3 feet long, sat on a boulder, sunning himself beside our path. My dad and I talked about staying overnight in these empty villas, using our mosquito net and hammock. However, we knew it was too early to stop for the day. To add to our misery of walking miles out of the way because of man-made obstacles, we walked right into a construction site, probably for a future all-inclusive resort. Sometimes, these man-made obstacles were stone or cement walls that protruded out in the ocean, up to our waists, and we could not walk out into the sea that far with our backpacks. We entered the gates, hoping to walk through to the other side of the beach without being noticed.

A small but fierce Mexican security guard came after us. A machine gun was slung around his shoulders, and the weapon jostled while he ran towards us with impatience. He was adamant that we would have to walk around the compound; we complied because he meant business while hollering at us in Spanish. He pointed his gun at us when he met us face to face.

After our unpleasant encounter, we continued south, heading toward our destination for the night: the pueblo Xpu Há. Around 4:00 pm, after hiking for seven hot and sweaty hours, we arrived on the outskirts of the pueblo. Blisters formed on my feet, and sunburns covered the rest of my body. My dad was almost black from the sun. However, we soon forgot all of our minor discomforts as we walked up to a beach bar on the edge of the water and discovered that the bartenders would take cash. We enjoyed fruity mixed drinks and pineapple juice, swaying on bar swings and practicing Spanish with the locals. That was more fun than having a security guard pointing a gun at you, but that was all part of the adventure for the day.

While resting, we attempted to get information on places to stay overnight in Xpu Há, but without much success. The beach campground next to the bar was full. The bartenders suggested Copacabana, so we headed out. After walking half an hour, we found the "cabanas," but it was an all-inclusive resort that cost $250 per night. We returned to the beach bar, and my father searched the beach looking for other options while I stayed at the bar asking the bartenders. They told me that we could sleep under the palapa roof of the bar once it closed. I thought that was a good idea, but my father returned with news of a small hotel called Villas Caribbe for $80 a night. We settled on that even though there was no hot water, and we did not find the owner too friendly. The rooms were clean, though.

After checking in at Villas Caribbe, we noticed another beach bar near the property. There were three older Mexicans closing the bar, one of them climbing on a ladder up a palm tree to reach coconuts with a machete. Two of the gentlemen were around 50 years old, wearing baseball hats, shorts, T-shirts, and sandals. The other one was older, perhaps in his 60s, wearing pants and sneakers. They were all jolly and friendly and always smiling. I immediately saw this as an opportunity to make friends and practice more Spanish. I approached the three Mexicans, greeted them in Spanish, and asked if I could have a drink of the coco water. I reached in my backpack to show them my machete and quickly explained that we were walking from

Cancún to Belize. This got their full attention, and one of the men put down his machete and opened the coconut with mine while the other two Mexicans retrieved a glass and ice from the bar.

The oldest of the three men poured the coco water over the ice and handed the refreshing drink to me. He chopped the coconut in half to expose the meat. In all, they had about 10 coconuts for eating and drinking. He gave me the first coconut with a spoon, but the meat was hard. However, the second one was soft and jiggled like jelly, perfect for enjoying the sweet, cool meat. It had the consistency of Jello, and it was smooth but milky white. The Mexican men and I continued chatting in Spanish about where I was from in the States, and we exchanged our names. I showed them pictures on my phone of my family and my Siberian husky whom they thought was very pretty. "Ooo!" they exclaimed. "Ahh!"

When I mentioned New York, they knew where Maine was located. Unfortunately, they did not have any pictures to share. Our short friendship ended with me giving out postcards of Maine to each of them. I had postcards of Maine wildlife and scenery, such as moose, lobsters, loons, snow-filled fields, deer, and black bears.

I will always remember this lovely and most satisfying moment.

My evening at Xpu Há ended perfectly with a dinner at the Villas Caribbe's restaurant, which was on the beach in the sand. It definitely had a tropical and romantic atmosphere, and maybe someday I would bring my significant other to this exact spot. My dad and I shared a plate of grilled fish that were freshly caught from the waters of the Caribbean Sea, and the fish was accompanied by a baked potato with sour cream, salad, bread and a cold Coke. We were surrounded by little white lights wrapped around palm trees, rhythmic waves rolling in from the ocean, island music, and a gentle sea breeze.

But tomorrow would be another 15 to 20 grueling miles of dirty, hot, and sweaty adventures on the Yucatán coast. Our goal for the next day was to walk from Xpu Há to the small snorkeling condominium community named Akumal.

We awoke at 6:00 am and started walking at 6:30 am. It was best to start walking early in the day before the sun got too hot and knock off six miles. I quickly became accustomed to the weight of my backpack and our routine, although during the first two days, my legs were so sore from walking in sand and over rocks for 20 miles that I could not walk up and down stairs at all the next morning. And of course there were the sunburns. My father just chuckled and called me "spleeny"—he knew I loved every minute of it. Advil did not help, the only thing that did was to walk it off the next day. By day three, my legs were no longer sore, and I had started to tan.

Since the Villas Caribbe did not offer breakfast this early in the morning, we ate some of our trail mix and drank our water from the previous day. We decided to stop at the first place we saw with breakfast available. Unfortunately, we soon realized that was not a good decision.

Yet again, the problem was too many all-inclusive resorts and no Mexican cafés on this part of the coast. After walking for at least two hours, my father and I were desperately hungry for breakfast and something substantial. Not to mention, severe thirst was setting in. I also wanted and needed coffee. We repeatedly approached the loyal, stubborn, and unfriendly laborers that cleaned the beach early in the morning for the resorts, but they did not have the authority to serve us breakfast. They did not believe that we walked from Paamul, and they did not understand my simple Spanish. In fact, they were quite angry that we were walking on the clean beach of their employer. I felt they were angry because we put them in a situation that might get them fired.

So, we put our heads together and thought of a plan to get some food.

We came upon an open air resort restaurant on the beach that was serving breakfast to their guests. My father took his usual part of hiding with the backpacks while I sat at the bar that happened to be closed but had male waiters bustling around. I did not take notes for my journal or pictures as it was a desperate time; therefore, I do not remember many details. The waiters stopped at the bar often to fill up the orange juice glasses of the tourists. I asked a couple of friendly Mexican waiters if we could buy some breakfast. They seemed to want to help, but had no authority to grant or deny my request. We had never tried this with food, only much-needed drinks. I was concerned about our filthy attire and general wild appearance. We were becoming scummy, dirty, and smelly. Our clothes were never washed properly during the 8 to 10 days that we hiked each year. There were sweat stains under our T-shirts as my father never carried deodorant on these hikes, and my long hair looked like a rat's nest because of the sea salt; all of our clothes were covered in dirt.

One sympathetic waiter got the manager for me, however, and I explained our situation. The handsome English-speaking manager with flawless skin, a strong jawline, and dark mysterious eyes was very helpful and accommodating. He served us eggs, toast with jelly, one orange, and a coffee. The cooperative manager was even interested in hearing about our journey to Belize and seemed to believe me. He did not want any money, but my dad and I left some on the bar because we were overjoyed to receive hot food and cold drinks.

On our way to Akumal we walked by a huge coconut plantation, another small Mayan ruin, and a coati that was foraging quietly among the rocks on the beach. The coati was minding his own business and did not care that we were walking in his territory. Coatis are mammals related to the raccoon family, and their paws are double-jointed and can rotate enough for them to climb down the tree head first. The coati was looking for food scraps at the tree line on the rocky beach when I noticed a ruin. The ruin was rectangular shaped, made from limestone rocks and in very good condition. I imagined the small ruin was the same ruin that Peissel walked by on his way to Belize. We snuck through the barbed wire and explored inside. I did not find any paintings or sculptures, but I vividly remember crossing paths with what looked like a sea snake coiled in the shallow seawater among coral. The creature had black spots and its body was brown, yellow and beige shining from the sun. However, upon further research I learned that there are no sea snakes in the Caribbean Sea. What I saw was probably a beautiful gold spotted eel.

The terrain was challenging for the next 15 miles between Xpu Há and Akumal with alternating coral boulders, soft sand, or flat rock that resembled the moon.

But the things we saw and experienced were well worth it. I walked by a small ruin that projected into the sea, and I felt as though I was lost in history. Today, this is the site of a new resort called Grand Sirenis. I remembered Peissel hiring a Mayan Indian to assist him in carrying his bag further down the coast in 1958. The Mayan was named Miguel, and he lived in a hut near a small ruin on a large rock extending out into the sea near Xpu Há. They sat together, facing the sea and drinking coconut water, and eating horrible fish stew and tortillas. Of course, the hut is no longer on the beach, but the small ruin remains.

As we started out on the beach each morning and I lifted my pack on my back, I kept telling my dad, "When we get to the next town, I am going to find some 18 to 20 year old Mexican boy to hire to carry my backpack just like Peissel did." For miles, while walking over rocks, I repeated to myself how to ask for a young man to carry my backpack in Spanish. When I once asked a local if it was possible to find someone up to that task, he thought I could. But I never did.

Not only was it rocky in this area, but like any beach in the world, one finds debris washed up on shore. We saw items like rubber flip flop soles, tons of plastic bottles and broken pieces of plastic in all colors, the body parts of dolls, torn fishing nets, frayed rope pieces, parts of soccer balls, and sometimes household goods. The Yucatán coastline was no exception in 1958 or today, and most of this trash is not from locals, but washed ashore from other places. One of my favorite stories that Peissel tells is when he found an old light bulb lying on the beach with the word *France*, which made him extremely homesick. Luckily for him, while he bent over to study this light bulb, thinking of the civilization that it symbolized, he was hidden behind a rock from the three murderous men that escaped prison, looking for him because they wanted his expensive camera. My father and I found our share of debris, some of it natural, including hairy coconuts. Every time we would see these washed up coconut 'heads' onshore, my dad would call them Wilson, referencing the movie *Castaway* with Tom Hanks.

Early in the afternoon, while making our way to Akumal, we encountered our next obstacle, a large remote inlet about 200 feet in width. The seawater was too deep to wade across. At the far end of the inlet, there were too many mangroves and swamps to walk around. Besides, that would have added more distance. There were no people or settlements with boats nearby to ask for help.

My father declared, "We will need to make a raft!"

"*What?*" I exclaimed, and my heart started to beat faster.

An old pallet had washed onshore, and my dad immediately set about finding a large buoyant log to stick through the pallet to make it float. At the same time, I anxiously took all of items that could not get wet out of both of our backpacks—my camera, our money, our plane tickets, our passports, the maps, our first aid kit, and food—and I placed them in double Ziplock bags. I tucked all of these bags into one backpack and wrapped the whole thing in trash bags while securing it with a tie. The other backpack had the remaining items such as clothes, mosquito nets, and knives. I also started picking up old palm fronds that I found in the jungle shed by palm trees. I placed them on top of the pallet so the backpacks would not fall through.

We proceeded to test this crafty raft made in about 15 minutes by having my dad swim across first with the backpack that carried the nonperishable items while he pushed the raft along.

Halfway across the inlet, he yelled, "The current is very strong, but I can make it across!"

He then came back for me and the last backpack. We started upstream of where we wanted to land because the current pushed us downstream, but we successfully crossed to the other side without a drop of water in the backpacks.

This was the number one highlight of walking from Cancún to Belize for my dad. We were both very proud of his inventiveness.

Without any relief, we encountered the next obstacle: Yal-Ku lagoon.

But this time, it was people that gave us trouble. Yal-Ku lagoon is an upscale snorkeling park near the condominium resorts in Akumal. Underground rivers merge with the sea, and the water is surrounded by flat, solid limestone to form a great place for snorkeling. At the entrance, there is no beach; there is only open ocean water. Therefore, we had to walk around the public park that was occupied by many foreigners and upper class Mexicans on vacation. I could tell that this was kind of snobby by the expensive condos, fashionable swimwear and jewelry, and lots of colorful swim toys.

As we walked around the lagoon, the water was clear enough for my dad and me to spot the colorful, tropical fish. We also caught sight of a beautiful red and yellow Sally Lightfoot crab that was partially submerged and clinging to the side of a limestone wall. Peissel described this place as being rich in a variety of sea life, including manatees in 1958. However, I did not see any of those large marine mammals.

My father wanted to find a shortcut around the park, so he attempted to ask one of the swimmers if we could borrow her Styrofoam floatation devices to float our backpacks across the short distance to the other side. But she did not speak English, and she wanted no part in helping us. In the meantime, I took my time balancing around the sharp rocks, and as I put my foot out to reach the next rock, I found some of them slippery with brown algae. Consequently, I slipped on the slimy plants and went down with my backpack.

Luckily I did not get seriously hurt or wet, only scraping my leg.

About halfway around the lagoon, the staff employed by the park came running towards us and yelled that we could not continue walking in the park without bracelets. We repeatedly explained that we were walking from XCaret, but they did not want to hear any of it. They were not accommodating at all, even though we were almost half way to the other side. We ended up exiting the park through the jungle to find a path that led to Akumal. Even though the staff had distressed us, I was relieved to rediscover civilization and finally reach Akumal after our raft ingenuity.

Towards the end of the week, Dad and I wanted to do something different, and having discovered that Yal-ku lagoon was a great place to snorkel, we went back to Akumal. However, because the staff at the Yal-ku park irritated and angered my dad while hiking, he made me purchase our snorkeling equipment on the beach in Akumal and swim from the beach in the open seawater without paying the fee. I snorkeled in this lagoon, but found that Akumal's Half Moon Bay had a larger variety of interesting sea life, including many sea turtles (I can see why this beach is named Akumal, which means *turtle refuge* in Mayan), large fish, and fascinating plants.

After arriving in Akumal, we found an enchanting little local hotel named Qué Onda with rooms for 60.00 USD per night, including hot water, a swimming pool, tropical gardens, free use of bicycles, washcloths (which were nonexistent in all other local hotels) and thatched palm roofs. Qué Onda is one of my favorite Mexican hotels because of these amenities. Our room had fresh cut flowers, a psychedelic star light from the 70s, and the dining area floor was coral. Unfortunately, it is closed now. Akumal also has one of the best Mexican cafés, Luncheria Akumalito. The fresh squeezed orange juice, huevos rancheros, tortillas, salsa, and coffee are outstanding, and the prices are cheap.

Something that I routinely did while hiking from Cancún to Belize was, during each meal, I packaged my leftover tortillas in napkins and placed them in my backpack, saving them in case of emergencies. While exploring Akumal, we also went to the local tienda to purchase some breakfast food for the next early morning start on the beach. We bought cartons of pineapple juice, croissants, packaged Oaxaca cheese made in Mexico, raisin bread, and hot cross buns.

Typically, the pueblos along this stretch were divided into two towns. One was the coastal tourist town on the beach side. On the other side of Highway 307, you will find the local town, the 'real' Mexico. I would often go to the other side of the highway with my dad, as we did in Akumal, on that bikes that we borrowed from our hotel, looking for tamales and other unusual things you would not see on the beachside. The difference in the way of living is obvious. Instead of the grand condos, resorts and hotels, you see stucco buildings, huts, shacks, streets filled with Mexican people going about their life, and taco carts with home-style cooking. We could hear the local Spanish rap and hip hop music, and we could smell the rotating pork taco meat with lime juices; they were just waiting to be wrapped in freshly made tortillas.

After leaving this interesting little pueblo and eating our simple breakfast, we continued our hike south to XCacel. We passed some beautiful and pristine sandy beaches. There was a sand sculpture of a dolphin laying on its belly, the nest of a sea turtle with a sign made of sticks and cardboard that read "Do Not Touch," another large iguana, and a military post that was occupied by three men. My dad's biggest worry during this 550 mile walk was the military along the beaches because of the potentially dangerous situations. Almost every 30 miles, we saw military posts at the edge of the water, and they were often occupied by three men in uniform, complete with military helmets and machine guns. They were looking for drug packages floating in the seawater. Locals call these packages "square fish."

As we trudged on to XCacel, the sun was intense, and we took a break at the edge of the jungle in the much needed shade on the sandy beach. I often tied my wrap-around scarf around my head like a pirate bandana to protect me from the sun. My dad said that I should be on the television show *Survivor* because I looked like the contestants. We knew we were coming upon some desolate areas, so we stopped at an all-inclusive resort to "beg" for two cold Cokes.

When we rounded the next point, we discovered a beautiful deserted bay, one that would be great for being stranded. There was a moored white catamaran that sparkled in the bay. The catamaran was being rented by tourists from Massachusetts. After making friends with these fellow New Englanders and telling them our story, they invited us onboard for fish tacos and cold beers. We did not accept the offer for the tacos, as we were trying to get to our destination of XCacel before sunset, but we did drink the refreshing Dos Equis! And I must have drunk it too heartily and with gusto because, once we continued our walk along the beach, I broke or badly bruised my toe on small coral rocks. I was able to continue walking for the remainder of the hike, but I walked with a limp.

It was in the afternoon, after we walked along the beach and neared the edge of the jungle, when we reached two rather large circular stucco buildings with thatched roofs. We did not see any roads, other buildings, homes, or people outside. XCacel was on our topographical map as a "town," so we entered one of the buildings and asked a señorita if we were close. She told us that this *was* XCacel. We then asked her where we could obtain some purified water, food, and a place to stay overnight as we were getting tired.

She told us that none of that existed in XCacel.

The town consisted of those two buildings, and that was all.

We later learned that XCacel is known as a refuge for the nesting grounds of sea green and loggerhead turtles. Maybe it is a town for sea turtles and not for people. The beach is also well-protected in the interest of the environment and endangered animals, such as the bell snake. We were disheartened that we could not get something to eat and drink here, but we found a rustic lean-to on the beach that we used as shelter and rested. We ate some of our trail mix and drank our hot bottled water for lunch.

We had now hiked 15 to 20 miles in one day, and we had walked a total of 60 miles in almost 3 days. We were running out of water, and our bodies were sore, tired, and sunburned. I had blisters forming on my big toe, so I protected my toe with gauze, band-aids, and then wrapped my whole toe with duct tape so the bandages would not come off in the seawater. That worked wonders for an hour or two. When we hiked the beach, I either wore my Tevas, sneakers, or was barefoot. I never got a stress fracture nor were the bones in my feet sore from walking so many miles barefoot in the sand. I would have to wear my Tevas over the rocks or coral, but when the terrain changed to sand, blisters would form from the sand getting inside my Tevas and rubbing against my feet. When I started getting blisters, I would have to switch to my sneakers, which were very burdensome when the terrain switched to sand again. It was not that easy to put on and take off shoes while wearing an 18 pound backpack.

My dad always wore his Tevas and never got blisters.

After our break, and because there were no amenities in XCacel, we had to press on towards Tulum.

The terrain was once again a rocky shore. Along the way, I passed the cutest and most perfect bright green plant that grew surrounded by shells and pink coral pebbles. The shiny leaves resembled the wavy petals of a flower. Close to the plant was a huge piece of brain coral. It was about the size of a tire, and the surface of the fossil was a complicated maze.

Around 4:00 pm, we spotted a huge tower with a banner containing the words "Xel-Há" right on the rocky shore. We started to become worried about security in this popular snorkel park and beautiful natural aquarium. However, no one enters this inlet by way of the rocky coast. Xel-Há has a turquoise lagoon, a gentle river, and a thick jungle that meets the sea. The entrance to this inlet has a gap in the limestone coastline that is about 100 feet wide. Rocky cliffs, about 15 feet high, line the shoreline. The bay is Y-shaped, and tiny islands dot the bay of Xel-Há.

In 1958, Peissel had to walk around this lagoon, which added about ten miles and took an additional five hours of walking at night. But today, because it is a public and sometimes crowded tourist eco-park, there is a suspended foot bridge built across the lagoon. We only had to walk to the other side. However, we had entered the park illegally. Most importantly, it was late in the day, and we were hungry, tired, and out of water to drink.

While walking across the bridge, the seawater was so clear and vibrant that I could see many fish such as the Sargent Major damselfish, which are black and yellow striped. The fish were in a school and probably looking for food since I heard that tourists like to feed them frozen peas. Once on the other side, we proceeded to walk on the park's jungle paths to find the beach. As we were getting deeper in the jungle, there was no beach in sight, only more jungle, and the terrain was becoming rocky with cliffs, so we had to make a decision:

Do we keep going and hope to find the beach on the other side of this park to continue our walking? Or do we turn around and walk through the park, exit through the security gates, and get a ride just a couple miles south to Tulum? We could stay there overnight and then walk north to Xel-Há so we did not miss this section.

I opted for the second plan because I was worried about not having water, and it would be dark soon. The tricky part was sneaking past the exit gates without security noticing that we were not wearing bracelets. Sure enough, however, they stopped us. We lied and told the security guards that we had cut off our bracelets because of our sunburns and because the bracelets were too tight.

At first I was worried about what we were going to say and about lying. Were they going to believe us? Or call the Mexican Police and have us hauled off for interrogations about why we had snuck into this park to snorkel without paying? But then I thought that most people in this park had a lot of money, so they do not need to sneak in without paying. Most importantly, how many people snuck in because they were walking along the coast from Cancún? None!

So, chances were they would think nothing of our "sunburn and tight bracelet problems."

They believed us and waved us through.

Our taxi ride dropped us off in Tulum at a local, simple hotel named Acuario, which means aquarium in English.

We made it to Tulum, but we had our fair share of injuries and discomforts. Because of my scoliosis, I had pulled a muscle in my back when we left Maine, and the hotel owner graciously fetched me some ice, which is a precious commodity in these tropical parts of the world. I also had a broken or bruised toe, blisters wrapped in duct tape, scrapes, and a heat rash. My father had a seawater fungus foot from walking in too much water. The entire bottom of his foot was wrinkly and yellow with layers of skin falling off. While in our room resting, my dad picked off the dead skin and threw it at me from across the room.

I screamed like a little girl and ran to the opposite side, saying, "*Eww!*"

The thought of touching the dead skin and throwing it back at him grossed me out. He chuckled, inspecting his foot to see what he could do to make it go away.

After drinking all of the Cokes and ice water that we could find or hold in our stomachs, we explored the streets of Tulum in the pueblo. We discovered a spectacular meal of the most scrumptious barbecue chicken tacos, complete with homemade authentic hot sauces and corn tortillas. We even found a small concrete building behind a bus station with "Tortilleria MICHOACAN" spelled out in yellow and green letters. It was a tortilla factory with about 4 employees. One of them looked like a boy aged fourteen. His job was to stack the tortillas 18 inches high as they came off the machine. The workers stood proud and serious while I obtained permission to take photos of the Mayans with their prominent Indian features, their high bridged noses, jet black hair, and dark skin. The modern features of the teenager, like his spiked hair, clashed with the traditional features.

We lay in our comfortable beds that night with our bellies satisfied, knowing that across the street were the famous ruins of Tulum built on the cliffs. These ruins contain El Castillo, a famous castle that overlooks the turquoise sea; travelers see this ruin in the picturesque brochures that advertise Cancún and the Mayan Riviera. Before falling asleep, we discussed how we were going to continue walking the area that we skipped yesterday. My dad figured that it would be another 15 to 20 miles. We decided that we should now walk north in the direction of Xel-Há, but we would need to get across the steep cliffs that are 60 feet high and sharply meet the powerful waves on the sea. Before breakfast in the morning, we agreed that we would find a Mayan fisherman on Tulum beach who we could hire, with his boat, to take us across.

Tulum is a walled fortress with three walls. The fourth side is defended by the cliffs and sea. The Mayans used the compound for defense and as a religious compound. Zama, City of the Dawn, is the aboriginal name of Tulum. The main temple is called El Castillo, The Castle. When Columbus and the Spaniards approached the New World, they had only seen primitive Indians living in huts, and they were probably in awe and fearful when they spotted the city of Tulum, which rises above the cliffs on a summit. The Spaniards thought that they found the golden city of El Dorado because of the high amounts of obsidian in these ruins, which look golden when shining in the sun. Obsidian came from Guatemala, so archeologists believed Tulum to be a major obsidian trade center in Central America. Tulum was never conquered, but it was surrendered by the Mayans to the Mexican government in 1935.

When we awoke in the morning, my dad and I took showers, packed our backpacks, and checked out of the hotel. We immediately went to Tulum beach, stopping at a local market to fuel up on two fresh bottles of water for our backpacks. The first local with a boat that we approached agreed in Spanish to take us across the cliffs and drop us off at the nearest beach so we could continue walking. The man was wearing a baseball hat but had prominent Mayan features such as copper brown skin, slanted eyes, a long curved nose and round cheeks. He told us, in a business-like manner, that the price would be 100 pesos (ten US dollars) if we left immediately. However, we had not yet eaten breakfast. We talked him into leaving in 15 minutes, but he said that it would be 200.00 pesos. Perhaps he was in a hurry that morning to start fishing or he just wanted to make more money in the deal. He did not seem fazed by the fact that we wanted a boat ride around the cliffs. Perhaps he did not understand my English when I said that we were walking from Cancún. Either way, we were not able to talk him down on the price, but we were able to get a quick breakfast of scrambled eggs, toast, orange juice, and coffee at a nearby cabaña before we departed.

We approached the boat and carefully hopped in as the fisherman and his helper steadied the sides in the wavy ocean. My father and I enjoyed our boat ride on the ocean with the cool sea breeze and light salty spray; even at 8:00 am, the tropical sun was stifling hot and the heat made us sticky. As we traveled north, we gazed up at the castle and its outlying smaller ruins on top of the cliffs. From our viewpoint, it appeared that the famous ruin was in good condition with a taller structure in the middle flanked by two smaller ruins. I wished that I could have visited some of these famous ruins that we passed by, but we were on a different mission.

It was about two miles before we spotted a sandy beach on the other side of the cliffs. The Mayan slowly drifted his boat onshore and told us to hop out as his young helper passed us our heavy backpacks.

As soon as we said *adios* and *gracias*, I felt like I was stranded on a deserted island. To the right of me were high and ominous cliffs, and to the left of me was nothing but deserted tropical beach. The sixty-foot cliffs were comprised of razor sharp coral with a 45 degree angle, and the powerful waves were angrily crashing against them. The only hint of civilization in the forms of people and a motorized boat were leaving.

At the same time, my father had one of his great ideas. He brought me away from my stranded island vision by exclaiming, "Why don't we hike back along the cliffs to explore that last small ruin we spotted, the one that was in the middle of nowhere?"

I was game for any adventure.

Since no one was around, we proceeded to hide our backpacks in the jungle at the edge of the beach and used my small canvas bag to carry our important documents and money. We also took our water. I was a little apprehensive about climbing these cliffs because I could tell that this was going to be physically challenging and a bit scary, if not suicidal. If we lost our balance and plummeted to our dooms, not only would it be fatal, no one would know!

We took our first steps, and slowly, I gained confidence. I kept my gravity low while hanging onto the sharp rocks so I would not lose my balance. I had to keep looking ahead so I would know where to place my feet and hands to find the perfect spot to balance. My worst fears were of slipping and cutting my leg open, dropping through the rocks and bleeding to death, or falling head first on the cliffs then tumbling down into the turbulent ocean, never to be seen again.

In no time, my father was far ahead of me on the cliffs. Later on, he told me that he felt as confident as a mountain goat. As we were going along and getting closer to the ruin, I kept placing my hand in the crevices and cracks for stability. When my father turned around to check on me, he would advise me against doing that for fear of the poisonous spiders and scorpions coming out from their homes and seeing my hand as food.

After an hour of physical work and having burned 750 calories, we reached our goal. There stood the lone ruin on the top of the cliff in the middle of the jungle, which overlooked the Caribbean Sea. According to *Tulum, an Archaeological Study of the East Coast of the Yucatán* by S.K. Lothrop, this temple is structure 59.

Today, this temple is not part of the main attraction. Tourists are only allowed to visit the ruins inside the walls. In addition, tourists are not allowed to climb any of the crumbling structures, so it is more popular to take the paths that lead to the Tulum beach right below the cliffs. We do not really know how many people actually have visited this small temple, but I felt like we were only two of the few modern tourists that have done so. We were definitely off the beaten path!

The ruin was small, about eight feet in length and four feet wide: the size of a shed. It was preserved with a crowned honeycomb roof, which is not found anywhere else at Tulum. We ducked under the doorway of the ruin, expecting to see sculptures, wall paintings, or hand prints. I did not notice any wall paintings or sculptures inside, but I did see a hole dug in the floor of the ruin where archaeologists might have been looking for artifacts.

While standing beside the ruin on the edge of the cliffs, I viewed the beautiful cloudless sky, the blue horizon, and the sparkling turquoise sea with white caps. Behind me was the Yucatán jungle, loud with life yet quiet with mystery. Directly behind the ruin, there was a clear circular spot on the ground with a few large rocks where my father and I could rest. I imagined Mayan men in their loin cloths, wearing their beaded necklaces and war paint, sitting around a fire with their weapons in hand, and rejoicing after a successful hunt.

My father and I started to explore the jungle, but we decided to turn around when we noticed small cenote holes that were hidden within the floor of the jungle.

I cautioned my dad. "One of us might fall into one of these holes and break a leg. We aren't wearing proper clothing for jungle hikes, and I don't have my machete for cutting trails or warning harmful creatures of our approach."

My father agreed, and we said goodbye to this special place and walked an hour back along the cliffs, performing our balancing act for a second time.

At the end of this adventure, we were drenched with sweat. We had burned a total of 1,000 calories, were completely out of water, and it was not even lunchtime yet. We had not started walking our miles for the day, either! And we had to keep walking to find a settlement.

After finding our backpacks in the jungle, the first thing we did was go for a refreshing swim in the sea to cool off and rinse away our sweat. We hoisted our packs onto our backs, and we headed north on the sandy beach towards Xel-Há. It was not long before I started worrying about where we were going to find water on this seemingly deserted beach. How far would we have to walk—all day? I was so thirsty.

However, we were fortunate to find a large hotel under construction. We could hear equipment such as saws in use, so I cautiously went out to the back of the hotel to ask in Spanish if these men had purified water. While walking through the hotel dining room, I noticed the colorful walls made entirely of tiles with pictures of Mexican themes. The construction men brought my dad and me into a large cold room in the kitchen with jugs of ice-cold purified water. Such a sight brought relieved smiles to our faces! We drank as much as we could as we were very thirsty from climbing the cliffs.

We left the unfinished hotel, and because we did not have enough bottles to fill with water for the rest of the day, we soon had to open wild coconuts. This was our first of many wild coconuts that we had to open to sustain our bodies' needs. We found some that were within our reach, and they were young coconuts, perfect for eating because of their soft meat. I was surprised at how well they quenched my thirst, and I was also surprised at the coolness of the sweet coconut water, even though the tropics are so hot. I did not become sick from drinking the wild coconut water, and many times, the nuts were mostly green.

After our refreshing coconut drinks, we walked pass Dreams Tulum Resort in the afternoon, and after five more miles of sandy beach, we reached Tankah and Casa Cenote. Tankah seemed to be a community of small local hotels for tourists and vacationing Mexicans. Hidden jewels, history, and treasure hid inside the jungle. I learned that there were twenty three structures of Mayan ruins with shrines, tombs, and stucco figures in this area, including a cave containing a Mayan idol, and an altar. In 1958, Peissel described Tankah as a coconut plantation complete with a stone house, two tin-roofed sheds, and four palm huts, which seemed like civilization to him after the desolation of the coast that he had traveled.

By the time we approached Tankah, our clothes were filthy and smelly, especially my one pair of socks that I had been wearing with my sneakers because of my blisters! I felt and looked like a bag lady by the end of the week as we had walked over 100 miles. Everything I owned was carried on my back everywhere I went. I especially felt like a bag lady when I needed to wear my scarf around my neck because of the sun. My t-shirt was under my backpack straps because the straps hurt my sunburn. I walked with my camera pack around my waist, my backpack on my back, my sunglasses around my neck, and sometimes my sandals in each hand.

Here is where we rested and swam in the cenotes. We had heard stories from our Bed and Breakfast Inn about a large boa constrictor that lives in these fresh water pools. But when I went swimming, I did not see any snakes.

While resting at Tankah Bay under palapas on the beach, we met some older ladies and we told them that we were walking from Cancún to Belize. We showed them the pictures on my digital camera that I had taken from Paamul to Tulum, and they gave us some water and beer. As we were saying goodbye and I was attempting to lift my backpack on my shoulders, one of the ladies helped me and said, "Oh, you poor dear, you look a terrible wreck!"

The next day, we found the greatest seafood restaurant on the prettiest bay from Cancún to Tulum. Oscar y Lalo Seafood restaurant is located in Soliman Bay, about a mile down a dirt road from Tankah. My father and I had scrumptious dishes of Yucatec whole fish, onions and peppers steamed in foil, homemade tortilla chips and salsas, French fries, black beans and

Mexican rice. We were presented with a coconut shell full of coconut water, and pineapple juice mixed with rum with a straw for our drinks. After our lunch, we took a nap in the colorful hammocks provided by the restaurant. We swayed over the edge of the water, and the sea breeze kept us cool. The palm trees gracefully leaned over the Caribbean Sea as if they wanted to reach the waters and become one with them. The vibrant colors in the surrounding bay made me never want to leave this place.

Once we had a little rest in this tropical paradise, we slowly removed our sore bodies from our hammocks and explored the area. Soliman Bay has a clean local campground. There is a bonfire area with a circular shape, and it features large conch shells and an altar complete with candles. We walked north at the bay, and after just a few feet, we came upon nothing but thick mangroves, which stretched as far as we could see. Looking at our map, my father knew that around the next point of mangroves, after Soliman Bay, was a rocky shore and Xel-Há. We realized at that moment that we had made a good decision two days ago at Xel-Há to exit the snorkeling park and find a ride to Tulum. If we had kept walking that evening, we would have been forced to turn around because travelers cannot walk over mangroves.

After hiking our first section of 120 miles in nine days, it was time to go back towards Cancún for our flight home. To do that, we needed to get to the highway by walking on the dirt road and flagging down the bus while we waited at the "bus station." A typical bus station on the highway consisted of one small palapa and one plastic outdoor chair. That was where we waited for the bus, and alongside us was the largest iguana we have ever seen, four feet long or more, living inside a cinder block.

At the Cancún International Airport, I tried to linger outside as long as I could to soak up some more of the humid air before I entered the air-conditioned building that would lead me out of Mexico. Although I lingered, I did not want to miss my plane. When the plane took off north to the United States, I stared out my window to capture and save the image of the palm and chicle trees, the surrounding jungle, the beaches, and the Caribbean waters until we returned to continue our hike next year.

We had now completed the next segment of our walk from Cancún to Tulum, and we hiked a total of about 160 miles. Not only was I in love with Mexico, but now I was obsessed with finishing this hike to Central America, and nothing could stop me. Once I get an idea in my head, I am always determined to finish it. I set my personal goals high, and I never quit. Even though hiking in the tropics in a foreign country on the sand and boulders with an 18 pound backpack and no water or food at times was difficult at age 42, it did not seem like work to me because I was doing something that I love. Therefore, I knew that we would be successful.

CHAPTER 6

Tulum to Isla Punta Pájaros: The Mayan Curse and the Haunted Cabaña

• • •

WHILE RESEARCHING OVER THE WINTER of 2008, I found few obstacles for the next section from Tulum to Isla Punta Pájaros in our walk. These included the two large bays known as Ascension Bay and Espiritu Santo Bay, Boca Paila, the Punta Allen peninsula, Sian Ka'an (Mayan for *Where the Sky is Born*) Biosphere Reserve, and the private island of Isla Punta Pájaros, which is located between the two bays. By measuring the mileage using the topographical map, 120 miles would place us after Espiritu Santo Bay and Punta Herrero, and near Majahual.

However, it was becoming clear to me that I always underestimated the mileage because we did not reach where we wanted to be until the following year. I made notes that there are many small ruins in this section that Peissel explored, but because they were mostly inland and we were determined to walk as many miles as possible along the coast, we did not search for them. We would leave the popular tourist region and enter no man's land after Tulum. Even Bruce Concord, author of the *Adventure Guide of the Yucatán*, admitted to me that he "didn't go that native," as in going to Isla Punta Pájaros. The places that we would pass on foot were not places that anyone had researched heavily. Therefore, it was very difficult to find current background information and accurate descriptions; we only had basic geographical layouts to guide us.

The first obstacle was Ascension Bay, which is a large and open body of water. The entrance is about twenty miles wide, and the bay is perfect for world class fishing. Espiritu Santo Bay is somewhat smaller and is only passable by boat. After Tulum, our starting point for that year, there were no more all-inclusive grand resorts and no busy tourist areas until we reached the end of Mexico in XCalak, which is on the Belize border. We would be on our own. We would be traveling to Tulum, about three hours south of Cancún, by ADO bus.

At one time during our research, to get through all of this water, I told my mom, "We think that we want to purchase a light inflatable raft to carry with us. And I want to bring snorkeling goggles with us for hunting fish, so we can spear them to cook for food over the open fire on the beach."

My mother rolled her eyes and laughed at us. "You might want to bring a small flashlight."

I decided to not purchase a raft since that would have added weight. Besides, my father was sure that we would find a boat.

Boca Paila is a small inlet at the start of the 40 mile barren peninsula, which stretches to the small fishing community of Punta Allen. Punta Allen is the largest village in Sian Ka'an with about 470 inhabitants. The Boca Paila inlet is shallow during the dry season. I did not see a problem crossing this since there is a bridge downstream, but that would add more unnecessary miles to our journey. We hoped that we could wade across

Boca Paila if that the current was not too strong. It is also a popular guided fishing spot and features a lodge. I was worried about walking 40 miles in the tropical sun with only one lodge or settlement that could provide us with fresh water.

Sian Ka'an Biosphere Reserve starts after Tulum along the Punta Allen peninsula, ends about 15 miles after Espiritu Santo Bay, and stretches inland near the border of Felipe Carrillo Puerto with about 1.3 million acres of protected land. No resorts are allowed to be built in this reserve, and most places do not have electricity; they are only powered by generators that operate from sun up to sun down. The reserve was established in 1986 by law of the President of Mexico, and Sian Ka'an was also declared a United Nations Educational, Scientific, and Cultural Organization World Heritage Site. In addition to being a nature reserve for tourists who seek guides for nature walks, fishing, diving, snorkeling, and kayaking excursions, there are educational programs, and the scientists conduct research. Some of the research activities concern solar and wind generators, meteorology, water treatment, composting toilets, the sustainability of lobsters, the nesting of sea turtles, and the maintenance of plant nurseries.

Working with sea turtles and studying meteorology interest me while sea turtles and lobsters interest my dad.

The reserve is surrounded by inland swamps and faces the Mexican Caribbean with the Mayan Coral Reef, which runs all the way to Belize. Besides having limited drinking water in this reserve, I found out that travelers are required to get a permit at the security gate and pay a fee to enter. However, we would not be entering from the highway like normal tourists.

So, I asked my dad, "Do we check in with the possibility of being asked to go to the highway, pay the fee for entrance and a guide, or do we keep walking on the beach?"

He answered, "We keep walking on the beach."

Once my research was complete and early spring came in Maine, the excitement of our departure for Mexico and walking our next section was upon us. My dad and I left Portland, Maine and arrived in Cancún early in the afternoon. Before taking the ADO and MAYAB buses to Tulum for only 4.00 USD, we stopped in Puerto Morelos for a swim and a late lunch. We changed into our bathing suits in a concrete compound on the side of the street in Puerto Morelos and swam in the Caribbean Sea. We then enjoyed tamales at El Tios, and even my father ate them, probably because the inside was filled with only chicken, and the sauce poured on the top of the tamale was a simple yet flavorful tomato sauce. For once, he was not looking around for a cheeseburger joint. Lastly, we went to the Internet Café for dessert and had warm croissants with blackberry jam and tropical smoothies before starting our journey south to our starting point in Tulum for the next 120 mile section. I felt like we were becoming experts at walking the Yucatán coastline when some tourists in Puerto Morelos asked us for directions on the street. We must have looked like we had been in town for a long time with our backpacks, walking around like we knew the place.

We traveled like locals to Tulum, using the chicken buses, and arrived at Tulum Beach in the evening, at the point where we had left off last year. Our goal was to stay at Copal Cabañas, which was about three miles away, for the night. Because it was early in the evening and the coolest part of the day, we decided to walk along the large rocks and cliffs to Copal Cabañas. It was refreshing to hike in the evening, complete with a pink, purple, and blue sunset; there were dark limestone cliffs in the background. However, the weather was a bit windy, and the palm trees on top of the cliffs were swaying, but that was nothing compared to when we started hiking south in the Punta Herrero area, about a year away. It was invigorating to get some exercise after sitting on the plane and buses all day.

The most memorable parts of staying at Copal Cabañas was the door to our room, which had an elaborate carving of a Mayan King, beholding two rainbows in the colorful sky that overlooked cliffs and palm trees, and the unusual chance for me to take a photo of four military men in their complete uniforms. The latter was uncommon because the military personnel do not like to be photographed because they take their jobs seriously. In fact, some Mexican officials will shoot first and ask questions later because of the dangers of drug lords in other Mexican states. However, these men were friendly. I asked in Spanish if I could take a picture of them, and they nodded their heads. They allowed me to take photos while they posed in their army helmets and camouflages, and they were armed with their loaded machine guns while we stood on the cliffs. Every other time (and there were many instances) we ran into military men with their loaded guns on the common streets or parks, they never allowed me to take photos and were standoffish.

We were lucky that my mother suggested carrying a small flashlight because, when we awoke at Copal Cabañas at 5:30 am to start our day of hiking the beaches, it was totally dark. We quickly confirmed from my research notes that in the Sian Ka'an Biosphere there is no standard electricity from 10:00 pm to 6:00 am, and when there was electricity, it was produced by a generator. There were no hot and fresh showers. Basically, we would live primitively with a tent and no basic necessities in a foreign country for the next eight days. But that made these parts of the Yucatán coast more appealing and challenging for us.

After a yummy breakfast of tropical fruit, yogurt and huevos rancheros at Copal, it was time to start a full day of hiking, but not before my dad and I used our imaginations. Often times on the coast, I saw vines growing at the edge of the jungle, reaching down the beach into the water. I found the perfect vines growing on Tulum Beach and it reminded me of *The Ruins* by Scott Smith. In the horror and science fiction story, man-eating vines in the Mexican jungle attack tourists from Cancún who are on an archaeological dig. I laid down on the beach with the vines over me and feigned horror while my dad found some red flowers nearby that he picked and placed on the vines, just like in the movie. The picture that my dad took made a great story in my slide show for the kids back home.

As we headed out on our beach trail towards Punta Allen, we reached a small yoga retreat and cabañas within the first hour. The guests were practicing their getaway stress-free yoga exercises on the tropical beach. This excited my dad when he saw that the girls were exercising while plastering beige mud all over their topless bodies.

Our first few miles down the Punta Allen peninsula were most enjoyable with our unusual activities and sights, but that soon came to an end.

We started to perceive how difficult the next 35 miles were going to be. We had walked about five miles so far. It was 11:00 am when we became aware that the Punta Allen peninsula was so desolate that we wondered if we had passed the cabins where we had intended to stay. We kept walking through the unchanging and barren terrain. We wanted to reach the tent cabins of CESiaK (Centro Ecologico Sian Ka'an), which we thought were about six miles from Copal Cabañas. So, we should have only had one more mile to walk. We knew CESiaK was the only place to stay until we reached the outskirts of Punta Allen, at least 25 more miles, so we had no choice, even though it would be early in the day. We knew the Boca Paila Fishing lodge was located about halfway between Tulum and Punta Allen, but most world class fishing lodges do not allow guests to stay just one night. At that point, we realized that we must have entered the Biosphere, and we had seen no entrance gate with guards, so we had kept walking.

We decided that if CESiaK asked us about it, we would obtain permits.

As we kept walking along, we were entertained by the artful structures on the beach. A palm tree grew so that half of the trunk was almost parallel with the beach and the other half was angled 45 degrees upwards. My father climbed upon the trunk to pose for an interesting picture. I also took a photo of a palm tree with its roots flipped upside down, so that the roots looked like hair; someone had drawn a face on the stubbed trunk. Since it was Sunday, we passed by a Mexican church group enjoying a service on the beach, complete with upbeat songs and a baptism performed in the sea. What an inspiring place to hold a service!

Punta Allen Peninsula's width range is between ¼ and a mile long. Therefore, the dirt pothole-ridden road to Punta Allen is not too far from the beach, sometimes right at the edge. But there were high sand dunes blocking our view of incoming vehicles. It seemed almost impossible to climb the dunes because of the soft sand and vegetation on top. Even though there was no one around to help us if we needed it, and no food or water, the beach was spectacular with its blinding white sand, and it was perfect for refreshing swims.

Finally, we reached CESiaK early in the afternoon, just before the restaurant closed for lunch. CESiaK is an ecotourism and educational center with small tent cabin accommodations. The cabins are one of my favorite types of places to stay because they are very rustic, built with wooden frames, canvas walls and thatched roofs, with flaps for the doors and screens for the windows, surrounded by untouched tropical beauty. There were two twin beds against the walls. We essentially lived with nature, experiencing the weather and sounds. The weather was still hot and dry, but we could hear many insects—the crickets, mosquitos, and cicadas—strumming their instruments throughout the night.

My dad and I climbed the towers, which are made of tree sticks, and we got a clear picture of the narrowness of the Punta Allen peninsula. On one side of the rickety tower, you see the waves from the Caribbean Sea with a small strip of jungle and palm trees in the middle, and on the other side, you can see the swamps and mangroves. These are two totally different ecosystems that you can see at once, and the contrast is impressive.

We were reminded of our primitive surroundings at breakfast the next morning. As I was eating my pancakes in the restaurant, I found a medium sized red ant *in* my pancake. I can deal with an ant on my plate with food, and I can even deal with an ant on my pancake. But when an ant is *in* my pancake that suggests that the ant was cooked with it, and that means that more ants were probably living in the pancake flour.

I tried to push away my plate of pancakes, and my dad asked, "You're not going to eat that?"

"No," I whined. "It has an ant inside it!"

"Don't be spleeny," he said as he shook his head and took a bite from the pancake, "it's only an ant."

I imagined several hordes of ants congregating in the corners of the pancake mix, sitting in the container for months, and the minute they are discovered, I could see all of them scattering in different directions.

Consequently, I only ate fruit that morning.

We still had eight miles to walk before we would find the last place to get water and possibly lunch for the day: the Boca Paila Fishing Lodge. On the map, the lodge appeared before the Boca Paila Bridge. *Boca* (mouth) *paila* (Latin cooking pottery) comes from the fact that a *paila*, used by the old chicle tappers in Quintana Roo, was found at the mouth where the salty lagoon meets the Caribbean Sea. This lagoon area is also a world class fishing ground.

We certainly had enough to keep our minds off our growing predicament of entering no man's land. The beaches in this area were some of the most beautiful and remote. We enjoyed the swims that kept our energy up and our bodies cool. Along the way, we stopped to chuckle at a computer monitor that had been topped with a coconut head on the beach, in the middle of nowhere. My dad found a sea creature that I thought looked like a beige fragile egg with baby clams growing on it. I had never seen this odd animal before. Later, I learned that they were not baby clams, but Gooseneck barnacles. The larvae of these barnacles settle on floating debris. This species of adult barnacles are attached to the debris by a thick muscular stalk and is considered a delicacy in some countries because it is meaty and substantial.

To keep us occupied in the grueling heat, we pretended that we found a treasure of $100,000.00 in cash.

My dad asked, "What do you think I would do if I found a treasure like that on the beach?"

I answered, "Well, you can only claim about $10,000.00 on the plane back to the United States."

"Then I would hide it each year in the same spot and take $10,000.00 home each time, after splurging some of it on a rich resort with a lot of fruit daiquiris!"

"How are you going to make sure you know where to find the $100,000.00 each year?"

My dad never saw that as a problem, probably because he has been called a "walking roadmap."

I said, "You know, you could use some off-shore banking and deposit all of the money in international banks or hire a boat to take you to Florida with the treasure."

But that probably would not be as much fun as burying the treasure and finding it each year like a pirate.

On a more serious note, my dad was usually many yards in front of me because he was watching out for things ahead of us, looking out for the military personnel who search for drug packages, and pushing on to get around the next point to see if there was a town. The Mexican military and police made him nervous. There were military posts all up and down this coastline in almost every town. I think he was being a dad when he did this, and he was looking out for us.

At one point, I asked him, "Why are you always way ahead of me?"

He said, half-serious and half-joking, "I am watching out for danger, and you can't keep up with me."

I just mumbled something and kept on walking, but in the back of my mind, I thought it was his adventurous spirit that urged him to see what was around the next bend. It is like the old saying, "Anything goes in Mexico."

Around 11:00 am, we approached the Boca Paila Fishing Lodge; we found the owner Ricky and possibly lunch. While I hung out in the background, Dad got brave while looking a bit grungy, approached Ricky, and asked, "Could you serve lunch, if I pay cash?"

But Ricky, while trying to brush him off, said, "No, we only serve to guests of the lodge."

I got up my courage, went into Spanish-speaking-mode, took Ricky off to the side while smiling sweetly, and explained, "My dad and I are walking from Cancún to Belize, and there is no more food for another 20 miles. Would it be possible to make an exception?"

I must have conveyed our challenging and perilous situation because he went into his kitchen and asked his cook to make us something to eat. A few minutes later, a sweet Mexican lady stepped out of the kitchen carrying delicious ham and cheese quesadillas with fresh salsa and a dollop of sour cream on each triangle of the quesadillas, and ice cold Cokes, which she put onto our plastic patio table. The fabulous meal only cost $5.00 each. The cook at the Boca Paila Fishing Lodge even threw in some free bananas and oranges for our backpacks. However, there was no bottled water we could purchase here!

Whenever we ate on the trail after hiking and starving, the food always tasted the best, and we were most appreciative to get it. A simple lunch comprised of quesadillas or a 5 cent mango off of a Mexican farmer's truck is undoubtedly the tastiest food that I have ever eaten. Food always tastes better when we cannot easily access it.

We left the lodge and headed down the beach where we came to the Boca Paila Lagoon. We could see the bridge about 100 yards inland to get across the lagoon. But my dad thought that the water was shallow enough to walk across, so he started walking. I was nervous about carrying an extra 20 pounds in my pack on my back while crossing the waist high water, which could have a strong current. If I lost my footing and fell into the seawater, I could be carried away by the currents. While pussyfooting at the edge of the water, unable to make up my mind, a nice guide named Felipe appeared on a fishing boat, and he offered me a ride. I accepted.

As soon as I hopped out of the boat, I found a beautiful West Indian top shell, which was white with black stripes. It was lying alone in the soft silky white sand. It is named a top shell because it is shaped like a toy top. An interesting fact about the West Indian top shell is that the empty shell is used by Hermit crabs for homes. In Jamaica, the locals have beach parties where they race Hermit crabs who live in brightly painted top shells.

Another problem we dealt with was the drought and higher temperatures in the Yucatán that year. We noticed how dry everything was and how all of the greenery had a thin coating of dusty gray limestone film on it. The temperatures were constantly 108° F from 10:00 am to 3:00 pm while we were walking. It was overwhelming as we quickly lost our energy and became thirsty. This 40 mile stretch was probably the most challenging part in all of the 550 miles. Dad said that he wanted to rent a car for the rest of the week, and it was only Monday! The drought and heat were the first of many problems in this section.

We walked for about another 10 miles in this uninhabited territory. We had to conserve our water as we each had only one to one-and-a-half bottles left. The water was hot and not thirst-quenching anymore. I was becoming delirious with heat exhaustion and heat stroke. The terrain consisted of white sandy beaches, but some areas were small rocky coral beaches with protected bays.

To our surprise, at one of the rocky shallow coves, we came upon a local Mexican family having a picnic. We did not expect to see them because this was not an established park.

Where did they come from?

There were nine family members. They seemed very happy and were enjoying themselves. It was the perfect calm place to bring their babies and small children swimming. The family was just as surprised to see us as we were to see them. In Spanish, I conversed with them and told them we had walked from Tulum to Punta Allen. I knew that they thought we were crazy—I could see it on the faces of the men. They probably went fishing in these parts and knew the coastline to be barren. The family immediately asked us if we needed some water. They gave us their two gallon jug of purified water to drink, plus one or two bottles of water. But we thought that the best thing they gave us was the ice. How happy we were! We carried our jug of water and kept pouring it into our cups, which had also been given to us by the picnicking Mexicans, and we drank as much as we could.

Later on, we realized that this might have caused one of our biggest problems.

With another possible 10 to 15 miles to walk to civilization, and with the end of the day at hand, we had some decision-making to do. Since we carried our United States Army hammocks and mosquito nets, we attempted to find a clearing in the forest near the beach to make camp. I tied up my hammock on the nearest palm trees and tried it out. Because we had no experience with using hammocks or sleeping in them, we found that it was not at all comfortable. We could not lie flat, and the hammock was unstable. We discussed laying the hammocks on the ground and using the mosquito net to keep out the night creatures, and sleeping on the ground. Or we could walk through the jungle a few feet to the dirt road and hitchhike to the nearest cabaña, then walk the rest of the way to Punta Allen in the morning.

We agreed that we would let fate decide. We would go to the road, and if someone picked us up within two to three hours, we would take it. If not, we would sleep in the jungle.

Someone did stop for us.

Fortunately, it was an older Mexican guy driving a car with his wife and one year old granddaughter sitting in the back. Since we were strangers and probably looked very shabby, he let us know that he was in charge by demanding that my dad sit in front. I sat in back with his wife and the young child. After a few miles, we saw a somewhat old unprofessional sign with peeling paint that advertised "Restaurant Cabañas Fly Fishing Boat Trips." We paid the driver 10 USD and walked on the property, looking for the owner around 4:30 pm.

It did not take us long to realize that this place was no good, but we were stuck because we just could not walk anymore without rest. The first thing we noticed was that no one else was staying here, and I felt a little uncomfortable. The only other person on the property was the beady-eyed owner who acted like he was 80 years old, but he could have been thirty. He hunched over like he was sick as he walked towards us to introduce himself and see what we wanted.

He said in a raspy voice, "This is all I have."

The place was run down and the whole deal looked shady. We could not get any fresh water, cold Cokes, or pineapple juice! We asked to see where we would sleep. The cabaña was a typical round hut made of stucco with a thatched roof. There were two rooms each separated by a wall, but each room was just big enough to fit the small beds. The rooms were somewhat clean, but there was no generator or working lights. The shower was held up with electrical tape and wire. The owner did not speak

English, and there was no restaurant. The only table, where a restaurant might have been, was a rotten piece of plywood with a couple of barstools. The kitchen looked disgusting. The owner did tell us that he could make eggs and toast for breakfast. But with the greasy stained surfaces and the dried food splatters everywhere, we were not going to eat there. However, since we desperately wanted someplace to lay our tired bodies that night, we agreed to pay the 40.00 USD for the run-down hut.

Given that there was no restaurant, after our salt water showers, we locked up our backpacks in the room and started walking the few miles to the center of Punta Allen along the dirt and dusty road for dinner. We found a simple meal of soup, fish, and two drinks at the Cuzan Guesthouse and then walked back to our cabaña. While we were walking along the winding dirt road, it was completely dark. We were without flashlights, and there were bats flying around our heads.

We arrived back in our rooms, our stomachs were satisfied and our bodies were relieved to be lying down, but it turned out to be a long and scary night. Both of us heard rattling. We thought someone was coming out of the bathroom because of the moonlight shadows that were cast on the stucco walls. I thought the isolated owner was going to go Jack Nicholson on us. The wind was whistling so loudly that it made the windows slam open and closed all night. Since the hut was situated right on the beach, the sea breeze was strong. I have slept so many times on the beach that sometimes I find the monotonous rhythm of the waves irritating and loud, and not at all soothing.

Sometime during the night, as we repeatedly bolted awake, my dad said, "I had nightmares about coming home to a bulldozer in the yard with piles of dirt everywhere, and kids and dogs were in my house. There were also boys punching my granddaughters."

As I wiped the sweat off me and continued my tossing and turning, I exclaimed, "Oh no!"

We deemed the cabaña as haunted!

When we awoke at 6:00 am, the whole experience became even worse. The owner was up and about in his cabin, probably thinking that we were going to eat his breakfast. We heard him coughing up a lung and spitting up mucus repeatedly. I was totally grossed out. After brushing our teeth with tap water in the bathroom, we left that dive of a place just as quickly as we found it and walked to Punta Allen to find something good to eat for breakfast. One should consider the ramifications of sleeping in a questionable place like this.

After breakfast at Cuzan, we walked around Punta Allen that morning with our backpacks, hoping to find the American lady who owned an inn that might be able to help us. I read about this Inn and this "wonderfully nice lady" in a Yucatán adventure guide. Our plan was to ask her how we could get to the private island of Isla Punta Pájaros to hike, and where we might find a good place to eat lunch in Punta Allen, and if we could stay at her place.

We found her, and we discovered that she was very unhelpful and mean, and even hateful like a siren luring seamen to their rocky deaths. With the hairstyle and fashion of Peggy Bundy on *Married with Children*, she scowled and said, "It is not possible to go to Isla Punta Pájaros, and you cannot eat at my [place]."

She did not want us to stay at her inn. She did not want to hear me explain that I do slide shows for the public of Maine and that we were walking from Cancún to Belize, so maybe we could get permission to hike the island.

She interrupted us and declared, "We've already talked about this: no restaurant and you can't go to the island."

The people of Punta Allen had unhappy feelings towards this lady, which confirmed that our unpleasant experience with her did not have much to do with us. That is when we left that horrible place and went back to the Cuzan Guesthouse. Sometimes things just work out for the best because we met Lily from North Carolina.

Lily was the manager of the Cuzan Guesthouse with her Mexican husband, and she was just who we needed. Cuzan has rustic cabañas that were situated on the sandy beach and were only 35.00 USD a night. I loved our simple and comfortable room with a thatched roof because it had white mosquito nets hanging over the two beds. The communal shower and bathroom even had hot water, but it was saltwater.

The mosquito nets in the room reminded me of when Peissel was walking through these parts. Malaria is rare in the Yucatán presently, but adventurers still need to worry about it in wilder areas such as the South Yucatán. Even though it is widely known as a tropical disease, at its peak, it was present on every continent except Antarctica. Malaria is caused by a parasite that has infected the female mosquito, *Anopheles*, which bites humans and infects their red blood cells. Different species of parasites can cause different severities of malaria. The symptoms of malaria are chills, sweats, nausea, headaches, diarrhea, vomiting, and the sickness can rapidly cause death if not treated. Symptoms can show up within 2 weeks or up to one year after visiting a tropical country. A bite from one species of the parasite, *Plasmodium malariae*, if not treated correctly, can live dormant in red blood cells and flare up for decades.

After exploring the property and where we would sleep, we discussed our mission with Lily. She was so nice and accommodating when we told her our story. In fact, I found myself on the CB/Two-way radio talking with Tom, the manager of the Casa Blanca Fishing Lodge that is located on Isla Punta Pájaros. Lily connected me with Tom, and I started remembering my Navy days as I talked excitedly on the marine radio over the Ascension Bay. My dad and I wanted to include this private island as part of this walk. After I told Tom our story and that I was from the University of Maine School of Marine Sciences, and that I presented slide shows to the Maine public, he invited us to do a meet and greet breakfast with him at the lodge as well as visit the remote ruins on the island! In exchange, I was to mail him a CD copy of my slide show when we returned home.

Next, we had to figure out how we were going to get to that private island, which was 20 miles across Ascension Bay. Isla Punta Pájaros is considered an island because it is surrounded the Caribbean Sea in the front and the swamps and lagoons inland. There are only two ways to access this island—by air, using the private air strip, or by boat. Lily came through for us again. She knew a fisherman named Antonio who lived in Punta Allen. Antonio strolled over with his round belly, jolly face, Ixtapa

T-shirt, baseball hat, and red bandana wrapped around his neck, about two hours late, for our initial meeting and made a deal. But since we were all on Mexico time, we did not mind that he was late. He agreed to take us 20 miles across the bay, on a one hour boat ride. He would then wait for us on the island for most of the day while we visited the ruins and hiked. My dad and I speculated that he would fish while waiting for us, still making money. His price for hire was 150.00 USD, which we thought was reasonable. I felt very safe in the care of Antonio, and he was very professional. We would leave at seven in the morning.

With our new acquaintances, my dad and I discussed the dilemma of how to get across the second bay, Espiritu, after hiking Isla Punta Pájaros. This was not part of the deal, and the island is so remote and uninhabited that no one would be able to take us across the south end of the island to Punta Herrero. In addition, once we got to Punta Herrero, there would be nowhere to get food and water for another 30 miles. My dad and I agreed that, after we hiked the island, we would go back to Punta Allen with Antonio and hike the peninsula north to where we hitchhiked the previous day. Or we could rent a kayak in Punta Allen to explore the swamps and lagoons inland to look for wild animals. Locals had told me that, while they were fishing, they often spotted jaguars, barracuda, panthers, boa constrictors, crocodiles, foxes, crabs, monkeys, and black eagles.

For the rest of the day in Punta Allen, we explored the small fishing town using Cuzan's guest's bicycles. All of the roads in Punta Allen are dirt. When entering the town, the shacks are lined up along the road, with one small concrete building at the entrance where the police department is housed. There are no bars, hotels, or night clubs. The sleepy fishing village is quiet, charming and rich in culture. The population is 500 people, mostly comprised of Mayan descendants. There is a bread "factory" with a blue door that, if you knock on it, the baker will sell you a hot loaf of bread or a fresh doughnut for 15 pesos. There is one phone that everyone in the village shares, four tiendas, a colorful elementary school, and a playground with a basketball court. The locals make their living by fishing or eco-tourism. My dad went down a back road towards the swamps and only saw a green snake and lots of biting horseflies. We also went swimming and rested in hammocks in the afternoon. That evening, I became sick with what I thought was heat stroke and fever, but I managed to eat sopa de lima (Yucatán lime soup) before going to bed.

When we awoke at 6:00 am, I felt better. We met Antonio on the dock and prepared to leave for Isla Punta Pájaros. This private island is so secluded that I never found out who owns it. It appears that the Mexican government does not own it, so maybe it is independently owned. The first class Casa Blanca Fishing Lodge hosts VIP people and costs around $4,300.00 to stay for a week. The former president of Banamex (one of Mexico's largest banks), Roberto Hernández Ramírez, owns a mansion on this island. The president of Mexico from 2000 to 2006, Vicente Fox, also vacationed on this island. There was even an episode on the World Fishing Network on Casa Blanca, the remote ruins, and where to catch the most prized fish. In 1958, Peissel called this island Santa Rosa.

When we arrived at Casa Blanca, Tom had two place settings for breakfast on the dining table. He told us, "Order anything you want!"

My dad wanted an American breakfast of eggs, bacon, and toast. I loved eating the fresh tropical fruit such as melon, oranges, grapefruit, and lime. It was the first substantial meal that we had eaten in four days. After a quick tour of the lodge and conversations with Tom and other staff about our hike, Tom introduced us to our guide and truck driver who would lead us to the remote ruins named Tupac and Chac Mool. We were only allowed to visit these ruins with our guide, Chris. We were very fortunate to have been given a breakfast, a truck driver, a guide, the use of canoes, and a visit to the ruins on this island as guests of Tom. We were not going to pass up this opportunity of a lifetime. Chris also brought along his girlfriend to whom he had just proposed. The pickup truck driver loaded a cooler with cold drinks in the back for us, and we hopped in along with it. The dirt road was very bumpy as we were jostled when the truck went over rocks and huge potholes, trying to miss the lizards and other small wildlife scurrying across the road in the deep Yucatán jungle. It was not long before we arrived at a tiny dock in a muddy area at the edge of mangroves.

"I feel like Harrison Ford in *Indiana Jones*," whispered my dad as we paddled our spider-infested canoe through the swamps, trapped in the boat with nowhere to go, with our bare legs exposed, waiting to be bitten by the horrifying eight-legged creatures with eyes bulging at us.

Each turn through the twisted mangroves was like a maze, hardly wide enough for our canoe, while we followed our guides. As we got deeper into the swampy jungle, the air got hotter with the stifling humidity, with no sea breeze whatsoever. Sometimes my dad and I would spot a tributary off our main stream, look down the waterway and be tempted to turn our canoe to explore on our own. But we kept going in search of these ruins named Tupac.

Suddenly, as we turned a corner, we discovered the hidden Mayan ruin, Tupac. The shape was rectangular, and the ruin was about the size of a small house. There appeared to be a chimney on top and honeycomb windows. It is possible that Tupac was used as an observatory by the Mayan Indians to look out for enemies approaching inland from the jungle. There was a ladder made of sticks that we climbed to look out over the swamp for miles. The other interesting things to note were the small red hand prints and the Quetzalcoatl head statue left on the outside of the temple, possibly thousands of years ago! As we entered, we noticed there were many bats, spiders and iguanas now living inside the ruin. This structure is not mentioned in the report *Tulum, an Archaeological Study of the East Coast of the Yucatán* by S.K. Lothrop. It is also not visited by the tourists on the Yucatán mainland.

We left this peaceful historical setting and canoed our way back through the waterway tunnels to the little dock and truck to visit the next ruins, Chac Mool, on the island. These ruins were once a sacrificial Mayan site. Chac Mool is named after a statue that depicts a human figure lying on its back with knees drawn up and head turned to one side that is found at this site. Chac Mools have been discovered in other temples at Mexican sites such as Chichén Itza. The importance of Chac Mool statues is unknown. Chac Mools should not be confused with Chaac, the rain and thunder Mayan god. Chac Mools are usually found with a bowl or tray lying on its stomach to receive the still-beating hearts of the sacrificial human victims. The Chac Mool statue at these ruins on Isla Punta Pájaros was missing the bowl as well as the head. Chris, our guide, told me that the head was stolen. There was, however, a hole about the size of a heart in the chest of the statue. We found a sacrificial stone that Mayans used to lean the victim's body over to cut out the heart, and we also found temples, tombs and a metate_at this site.

A metate is a Mesoamerican tool shaped into a slab by hollowed-out stone. It was used by women to grind corn to make tortillas. Chris also told me that a body was found in one of the tombs and is displayed at the Museum of Anthropology in Mexico City. There was a structure with an entrance of about half the size of my father, who is six feet tall. I took a picture of him standing beside it to compare.

I left Chac Mool feeling very fortunate to have visited it and in awe after learning a little about Mayan history. But now it was time to hike this beautiful remote island. After the truck dropped us off at the south end and before we headed out on foot, we guzzled some cold drinks. While resting with our sodas, I started to feel sick with Montezuma's Revenge. Montezuma's Revenge is named after an Aztec king who eliminated his Spanish enemies with poison a thousand years ago, and his name is now invoked when tourists get traveler's diarrhea in Mexico from drinking tap water, eating tainted food, or staying in unhygienic places. After I used the bathroom, I felt a little better, and we started walking.

These 15 miles were the most pristine, wild, and peaceful tropical paradise in the entire 600 miles, and we found our favorite spot. You have to see the turquoise ocean, crisp blue sky, waves gently lapping the soft sand, and peacefulness of the deserted beaches. It was a special place where one would want to stay forever. We went for many energizing swims and breaks under the palm trees in the shade on this island while walking back to Casa Blanca. About halfway through our hike, we noticed that the driver of the pickup truck was sitting under a palapa roof on the beach checking on us. He then drove the truck along the road as we walked. We do not know if it was because he was concerned about us or because it was a private island and it was his job to make sure that we did not go off the beach and find something we should not find.

Even though these were the most beautiful beaches we had ever seen, it was also the most difficult walking. As we stepped one foot in front of the other, each foot sank about six inches deep in the sand, and the beach was at an incline for miles. We walked on the deep inclined terrain, and as soon as we entered the seawater, it was waist high. In addition, it was very rocky with sharp jagged limestone and large holes falling through to the seawater. We walked by a huge ship engine, which was rusting and was mysteriously stuck in the sand at the edge of the water. The engine was about seven feet high and about four feet wide with an old rusty wheel on one end. We did not climb on it for fear of getting cut on the sharp metal.

Even though I had Montezuma's Revenge, I still hiked the 15 miles, but not without being way behind my father the entire time. I was not vomiting, but my stomach had cramps, I sometimes felt dizzy, and I was extremely sluggish. I did not have diarrhea again during the island hike, but I wished I that could have just lied down and rested. When I made it back to Casa Blanca, my dad was comfortably sitting and waiting for me with pineapple juice in hand. He jokingly made a remark to me about drinking all of the juice, so none was left for me, and I jokingly gave him a not-so-nice gesture. I must have been feeling better and realized how hungry I was because, upon greeting Tom at the lodge, he asked what I would like and I exclaimed, "A hot dog and macaroni salad!" Of course, no one along this Mexican coastline has hot dogs!

We said our goodbyes, expressed our appreciation, and exchanged business cards with Tom as we prepared ourselves for the boat ride back to Punta Allen with Antonio. I promised to send Tom a CD of my slideshow, and I even did better than that: each student at my Old Town, Maine Elementary School presentation wrote him a thank you letter and mailed it to him!

During our boat ride, Antonio was gracious enough to travel all the back way through the swampy mangrove waterways in hopes of showing us some wildlife. The boat rides were always so refreshing and enjoyable compared to the monotonous walking over 550 miles of hot sand and rock. Upon docking at the Cuzan waterfront in Punta Allen, however, things started to go downhill for us.

The next morning, Montezuma struck my father with a vengeance. After taking two bites of his pancakes, Dad quickly retreated to our cabaña, overwhelmed with nausea and diarrhea. He went from his bed to the hammock, back to his bed, then to the toilet, then back to bed, then to the toilet all day long. He would not eat or drink. Because of his age and the fact that I have never seen my father sick, I was concerned. I was also concerned about the bubbles of skin forming on my neck. The bubbles were large, transparent, and squishy.

So, I walked to the Punta Allen health clinic. It was the most pleasant healthcare experience of my life. For a short waiting period, an unannounced office visit, exam for my neck, advice for my father, medication for the sun blisters, and an English speaking doctor, it cost a grand total of 17.00 USD!

On my way back to the Cuzan Guesthouse, I stopped at a tienda to get food for my lunch.

I wanted to try what the locals do and buy a single serving of ham and cheese to make a sandwich and have an orange soda. But there was no bread, so I walked to the home bakery to ask in Spanish for a small loaf. I walked back to Cuzan, sat at the plastic tables and chairs in the sand on the beach, and put together my sandwich. Because there were no single servings of mustard or mayonnaise, I poured hot sauce from the bottle on the table on the sandwich. My complete, fresh and delicious lunch only cost 15 pesos, or 1.50 USD.

My father was still sick, but he was drinking occasionally. By the early evening, I had talked him into walking down the dirt road for some mango ice cream. He thought that was a good idea, and he thought that it would taste good to him. When we returned to our cabaña, he immediately went to bed. I kept myself busy by washing my dirty and smelly clothes and hanging them out on some rope between the two cabañas, just like the

Mexican ladies do. I also drank some beers and chatted with the waiter, Jose, at the Cuzan restaurant. I ended the warm and humid evening by lying in one of the hammocks on the beach, swaying myself to sleep.

This was when it got really exciting for me! I noticed something eerie in the weather. Having no radio, the Weather Channel, or outside contact, I had no idea of what was to come. But I definitely felt it, and I still remember the conditions I felt. I laid there, exposed to the weather, in the complete dark, without a single star in the sky as it became extremely windy, like a tropical storm. It was like nothing I had ever experienced. After I retreated to our cabaña, I slept in my bed, listening to the rain. I guessed the drought was over.

Upon waking in the morning, my dad felt a little better and we ate breakfast at Cuzan. He ate some scrambled eggs, while I had *huevos mexicanos*. The weather had turned for the worst, and the sky was pouring buckets of rain. We were now in a fully developed tropical storm named Arthur. Because it was now Friday, towards the end of our week, we decided to pack and head towards Cancún. My dad wanted a cheeseburger, anyway. I would have liked to stay in Punta Allen while hoping the rain would stop, but that never happened.

Since we were in a tropical storm, there were no taxis, and Punta Allen was void of tourists with rented Jeeps, we hitchhiked to Tulum. My father was also not strong enough to walk the 30 miles. There is only one way out of Punta Allen, so we waited with our soaking backpacks and clothes near the exit and entrance in the pouring rain while hoping that someone would drive by. Soon, we heard a faint hollering and realized that the voice, muffled by the rain, was calling to us.

"*¡Hola!* Would you like to wait inside?" a Mexican man shouted through the rain.

This thoughtful man was named Gerardo, and he was a guide from the Palometa Club in Punta Allen. He did not know us, but he took us into his home during the tropical storm and gave us his kids' Tom and Jerry and Spiderman towels to dry off. It was fortunate that I met this guide. He shared a wealth of information about the coast such as how to use natural plants found in the Yucatán for health remedies. He gave me rare seashells from his collection to bring back to show the kids in Maine when I do my slide shows. My favorite shell he gave me was orange, striped, and very smooth. He told me about this vine with purple flowers that is used to make tea and cure intestine illnesses. But I cannot remember what the name of the flower was because he was too good looking and I was distracted. We were equally impressed with each other's stories about the Quintana Roo coastline.

Because my dad was keeping track of cars going out of Punta Allen towards Tulum, he noticed a Toyota SUV, and the driver Charlie stopped for him. I said goodbye to Gerardo and hopped in the truck with my dad. Charlie was half Mayan, and his wife was from New Hampshire! On our way to Tulum, we chatted about many things. His wife loves to read Stephen King novels and about the crabs that invade houses in Punta Allen during the rainy season. As we were driving down the dirt road, there were many land crabs to dodge.

Charlie explained to us that when there is so much rain that all of the crabs enter the houses and congregate into one corner because they do not like the rain as the water fills the holes they live in. There are sometimes so many crabs that one cannot see the floor in their house! The crabs are generally bright blue with huge bulging eyes. They move creepily like spiders, and the largest one I have seen is about seven inches in width.

We also drove by some ruins on the side of the road, and Charlie stopped so I could take pictures. Some of these ruins were the same as the ruins that Peissel saw and described in 1958. At one point along the Punta Allen road, we saw a fallen shiny gray tree trunk that looked exactly like the Tin Man in *The Wizard of Oz*, and it looked like he drank too much Mexican tequila! It was a complete figure with arms, legs and a shiny metallic finish, worn from the tropical sun, wind, and sand. Upon arriving in Tulum, we thanked Charlie and invited him and his wife to Maine for a lobster feast, and offered him 20.00 USD. He did not want to take it, but we insisted that he buy something for his daughter with the money.

We travelled the rest of the way to Cancún for our flight home like the Mexicans do: by local buses. This 100 mile coastline stretch was definitely memorable for us. This was the only time we were ever sick during the 550 mile walk! Our sickness was *possibly* due to brushing our teeth with tap water in that haunted cabaña. But it could have also been contracted from the ice—probably made from tap water—that we received from the gracious picnicking Mexican family.

After I returned home, my skin started peeling badly due to the consistent seawater showers. It looked like I had leprosy. Large layers of white translucent skin would peel off, leaving red spots. Not only that, but within two weeks after returning, my father broke out with poison ivy all over his face, caught pneumonia, a catalytic converter fell off the shelf at the auto mall where he works and the resulting injury made him need 28 stitches in his leg, and I had a kidney stone. Nobody in my family has ever had kidney stones. and I am not prone to them. Perhaps our Montezuma's Revenge was due to the simple reasons above, but I cannot explain the other strange and mysterious events that followed our return.

When we visited the Chac Mool sacrificial site, did a Mayan God cast a curse on us?

CHAPTER 7

Punta Herrero to Punta Kanecaxh: A Mayan City, a Sea Monster, a Boa Constrictor, and Battling the Elements

• • •

Now that we have hiked Isla Punta Pájaros, we continued hiking the southern coast of Quintana Roo, called La Costa Maya (the Maya coast). This is a straight coast from Punta Herrero to XCalak—the end of Mexico—that is about 100 miles or more. The only obstacle that I had researched that winter was in El Uvero, which Peissel labeled as a bad land because many bandits lived in the area. I thought that this area would still be lawless.

In addition, I had made notes on various unique and strange objects, including lacquer stones and seeds called *ojo de venado* (deer's eye), washed ashore along this part of the coast. The interesting story behind the lacquer stones came from a ship that fell to its tragic death by crashing into the reef named Banco Chinchorro that runs along the coastline. The large cargo ship was carrying these clear stones when it ran aground and sank in 1942. Because lacquer is made from resin, the stones are light enough to float. In 1958, when Peissel was walking this part of the Yucatán coastline, he would find these stones every 500 yards because, for 16 years, the valuable sunken cargo would be shaken about by storm after storm. The floating stones would become loose and would be distributed along the Quintana Roo coast.

The deer's eye seeds may also be called hamburger seeds or sea-bean because they look just like a hamburger. The hamburger sea-bean grows climbing vines called *Mucuna* in the tropics. The seeds are used to make jewelry and decorations by the Indians. I purchased a necklace along our hike made with a hamburger seed, black nylon string, and brown and black wooden beads. If the lacquer stones or deer's eye seeds are found, they could be worth money. I did not find any of the lacquer stones, but I did collect many different seeds.

This year, we had an additional problem to deal with, and that was the swine flu. It was rumored that the swine flu started in Mexico. Therefore, most people I came in contact with in the United States tried to convince me that it was a dangerous idea to visit Mexico for fear of contracting the swine flu. Working in the healthcare profession, I received some sound advice from the local hospital which suggested that it would be perfectly safe to travel in Mexico. However, we did experience the effects from the swine flu while hiking the Punta Herrero coastline in an unimaginable way. But no matter the advice, nothing would keep me from continuing this adventure of a lifetime—the adventure of walking and experiencing the country that I had fallen in love with: the beautiful, picturesque, and exciting Mexico. I also enjoyed the privilege of traveling with my protector and adventurous companion, my dad.

For my dad and I, there were two ways to get to Punta Herrero, the southern part of the Yucatán. First, we could arrive in Punta Allen, hoping to find a boat, and sail across the two large bays of Ascension Bay and Espiritu Santo Bay with the private island of Punta Pájaros in between, hoping that the weather would cooperate. If the weather made travel by boat impossible, we could be stuck in Punta Allen or on the private island for days; this happened to Peissel. The second way to get to Punta Herrero would be to arrive in Cancún, take the local buses ADO to Playa del Carmen, and MAYAB to Felipe Carrillo Puerto. This would take about four hours and cost a total of 11.00 USD. Felipe Carrillo Puerto is mostly used as a connection point for travelers before moving on. To get to the southern coast, however, once in Felipe Carrillo Puerto it was anyone's guess how to get to the remote Costa Maya dirt beach road. There is one town on Costa Maya that the local bus travels to and that is Majahual, but they do not go further up the coast to Punta Herrero. We decided on our second option because we did not want the weather to possibly hold us up in Punta Allen.

Felipe Carrillo Puerto is a medium sized, non-touristy, non-English speaking Mayan city with a population of about 20,000 people. It is also situated on the edge of the Sian Ka'an Bio Reserve jungle. Most guidebooks and tourist internet sites write off Carrillo Puerto as unexciting with nothing to do. Out of all the coastal towns I have walked through, I became more infatuated with this small city than I did with any of the others. In fact, the next chapter is dedicated to Felipe Carrillo Puerto and includes an interview with a native whose ancestors are descendants of the Mayans from hundreds of years ago.

We arrived in Carrillo Puerto on an early Saturday evening, and we stepped off the bus with our packs securely on our backs; we were in search of a hotel named Chan Santa Cruz. My dad and I will always remember the funniest thing that happened next. Along the streets surrounding the bus station near the central park were taxis. One young *taxista* approached us in Spanish and offered to take us to our hotel. Since we were in a town where almost nobody spoke our language, we had not made any reservations and we had no idea where the hotel was located, we agreed. The *taxista* drove us around the park to the other side, parked, and asked for 15 cents. The hotel was located less than 100 yards away from the bus station! It was obvious to us that the taxi guy did not know that we had just walked from Cancún, and he probably thought we were like all other tourists in Cancún with their large and bulky suitcases, or he wanted to make as much money as he could. The taxi guy introduced himself as Luis Carrada and handed us his business card in case we needed his taxi services during our stay. My dad laughs heartily every time we think of the 15 cents that we spent.

Chan Santa Cruz was very comfortable at a rate of only 360 pesos (which is 36.00 USD) a night. We found that almost no businesses in Felipe Carrillo Puerto accept American dollars. The hotel was very clean, had an air conditioner, ceiling fans, free bottles of water, hot showers, and there was a satellite TV in our room. My father was very excited about the latter amenity because he wanted to watch the NBA playoffs before going to sleep.

During our first evening in Carrillo Puerto, we were very fortunate to stumble upon a festival and other cultural activities in the park. The Saturday night festival in the warm, humid, and thick air was complete with the cheerfulness of Mayan families. The children had lots of smiles and were jumping in balloon houses or riding on Merry Go-Rounds. In addition, there were battery-operated toy cars and decorated buses with neon flashing lights slowly moving through the streets while they blasted lively Spanish music. My dad and I strolled past the jazzed-up cars, the motorcycles and bicycles with fancy designs and fiery colors, pirates, and fantasy paintings. My favorite part was watching the bright-eyed Mayan children and the little girls with dark pigtails run around the park, laughing and chasing each other. They seemed so happy and carefree. I noticed one car was decorated in white bows and ribbons, and two white and gold swans made of cardboard sat on the front hood, implying that there was a wedding. I was brave enough to peek into the large and beautifully decorated church in the park and walked right in the middle of a Mayan couple exchanging their vows. The front of the church had a gigantic cross on the wall that almost reached the high dome ceiling, and the pew aisle leading to the front was decorated with ribbon chains and flowers showing the colors of the wedding: pink, purple, and white.

We encountered the taxi gentleman and his family at the festival. His daughter Xally was playing with other children. He introduced us to Catherine Gray, the wife of Xally's uncle, who is Mayan. Catherine is an American English primary school teacher in Carrillo Puerto, and she is the only American whom I have ever seen in this town. She proved to be very helpful later. Since there were no buses that travel the beach road to Punta Herrero, my dad and I decided to make a deal with Luis and take a taxi to the coast the next morning. The other advantage of taking a taxi is that we would get there quicker than taking a bus, which does not leave until later in the day. We enjoyed our Saturday evening at the festival, but it was getting late, so my dad and I decided we should get to bed because we would be hiking the coast tomorrow.

I could not wait to wake up in the morning and take a quick walk around this interesting Mayan city. Places are always different in the night than in the day. I arose in delight from a deep and dreamy sleep as I heard sounds from all sorts of animals that surrounded our room, and I remembered that we were bordering the Sian Ka'an Bio Reserve and the jungle. Whenever I wake up in a local Mexican town at 5:30 am, I love hearing the birds singing, the dogs howling and barking, and roosters cock-a-doodle-doo-ing, noises scattered throughout the small neighborhoods. They are such characteristic sounds for Mexico, and they were relaxing to me, like my very own live nature CD. The birds were loud and musical. One can sit in the park in the center of town on the edge of the forest in the early morning and hear a variety of birds singing and making sounds that vary between chatters, peeps, cries, shrills, and chirps.

After showering and gathering our valuables, we ventured around town looking for a place to eat breakfast. As we walked around town, it was very strange to see everyone staring at us, as there are no tourists, or Americans like my dad who towered over every Mayan. We found a local restaurant named Lonchería 25 Horas that serves fast and cheap Mexican food 24 hours a day. The open air restaurant was equipped with a small

12 inch color TV with wires hanging from the ceiling, and plastic tables and chairs. It was structured with wooden posts and a thatched roof. It is one of my favorite restaurants for its simplicity, character, and price. I ate Mexican eggs with ham, watermelon, bread, orange soda (it appeared that they had no juice), and coffee. Our breakfast for two was less than 3.00 USD.

We still had time to stroll around town before our departure for the coast, and I was continuously charmed. We took pictures of the colorful graffiti on the city's stucco walls, including one painting of an NBA basketball, which impressed my dad. The buildings were painted different colors such as bright yellow, orange, coral, pink, purple and all shades of green. The park, which is the central meeting place for children and families, is my favorite place. The streets are exceptionally clean and pretty, and the very old church and Cultural House, surrounded by palm trees and a statue of a famous Yucatán governor, adds character. The worn bricks, moldy cement, and peeling paint give the church a particular charm and mystery, almost like a European appeal because the building is so old. I imagined many Mayan Indians going to church throughout its history.

My favorite picture of all that I took is of an elderly Mayan couple sitting side by side on a park bench. The wife proudly wore a traditional colorful Mayan dress and her husband wore dark trousers and a clean pressed white dress shirt. They smiled as they agreed to have their picture taken.

We departed from Carrillo Puerto and the lovely park with Luis at 9:00 am. I always enjoyed the local transportation because I sat in front of the bus, collectivo taxi, worker's truck or family car and practiced my Spanish. On the way to the coast, we were stopped and searched by armed Mexican military, uneventfully. I think we were lucky that Luis was our driver because he was dressed in uniform and was local, and therefore the officials did not take advantage of us unusual tourists who carry backpacks with a machete. My dad and I arrived on our beloved coast in two hours. We asked Luis to drop us off at the Mayan Beach Garden Inn as we planned on making this our base while we walked the area of Punta Herrero.

After familiarizing ourselves with the inn, we secured a room for the night. I immediately fell in love with the colorful décor of this Inn, such as the striking Talavera sinks, prominent in the Costa Maya region, stairs with mosaic tile pieces shaped into a fish, and the lobby chair carved from wood into a jaguar with two heads. Sandy trails lined with shells weaved around the property. An over-friendly cat shared a hammock with me, sleeping on my lap. We ate lunch in the main dining room, overlooking the beautiful Caribbean Sea. It was the most delicious lunch I have ever had: a salad made of grilled tender chicken breast, avocado, romaine lettuce, pineapple, red onion and a creamy dressing served with sweet juicy watermelon and fresh tortilla chips with hot sauce that made me cry and sweat. My dad and I enjoyed our lunch with the sea breezes and beach sounds, and poured over the adventure travel books that were displayed in the lobby.

It was the most exciting collection of books I have ever seen besides the ones that I own. We picked up titles like *Sea-Beans from the Tropics*, *Lost Cities of North and Central America*,_and *Night of the Jaguar*. We stumbled upon an adventure guide of the Tikal National Park in Guatemala and discovered that the park has 222 square miles of rainforest trails deep in the jungle with many of the Mayan sites and jungle still undiscovered. This, of course, started a wildly excited conversation about our next adventures after crossing the Belize border.

After lunch, we discovered that Marcia, co-owner of the Mayan Beach Garden Inn, was the proud owner of the adventure books and was equally fascinated by *The Lost World of Quintana Roo.* We quickly became acquaintances, and she offered to arrange transportation for us to Punta Herrero, so we could walk south and be picked up by her at the end of the day at a certain spot. In order to cover the 30 to 40 miles from Punta Herrero to Mayan Beach Garden Inn, we had to hike for about three days. This appealed to us because we did not have to carry our backpacks.

Punta Herrero is an attractive small fishing village and appears to be much smaller and more off the beaten path than Punta Allen. The settlement mainly harvests and sells lobster from Espiritu Santo Bay. There is a small restaurant but no hotel. My father really liked this interesting village because of the fishing ornamentation and the remoteness, like a place from the past. I read that, at the end of the road to Punta Herrero, there was a small shack where an American couple named Walt and Lou had been living there since their yacht crashed on the reef. Unfortunately, we did not have time to explore the village because we had to start walking south to get to our pickup spot, which was the restaurant at Punta Mosquitero.

Since we started hiking along the shoreline in this area, the amount of interesting fossils we had discovered was fascinating. The different fossils appeared to be brain coral, star coral, sea fans, and some worms and mollusks. The geological age of these fossils, according to various geology websites, is two to five million years old. Since this was such a remote area, I wondered, as I stepped over the fossils, how many people have seen them. Did Peissel walk over these fossils? I also thought of the history of these animals that were once alive in the sea and wondered how many ships crashed on the reef off the beach here. Were there pirate ships? It is worth it to take a hike in the area for the day just to study the different kinds of fossils.

As we started to cover miles the first day, it was very windy on the beach. Marcia told us that the winds are the worst in the spring before the rainy season in June, and we were definitely exposed. After about five hours, we stopped at some cabañas to ask how much further to Punta Mosquitero. We also seemed to have picked up a companion during our stop. A dark brown dog with white paws followed us for two miles and he loved to play fetch. I would repeatedly throw anything I could find on the beach, such as medium sized round seeds, bottles, and small coconuts, and he would bounce along the sand at full speed and dive into the seawater or sand looking for the object. I liked it when friendly dogs came to greet us and then walked with us.

After three more miles, my dad and I stumbled upon the restaurant, and we shared a fried fish plate. These small restaurants along the beach often have no menu and the only thing to eat is a whole fried fish, complete with its head and eyes. One makes a taco by picking off the tender white meat and putting it on the handmade warm corn tortilla while dressing it with rice, refried beans, pickled onions, tomato salsa, mayonnaise that has been sitting on the table, hot sauce, and lime. I saw that the locals always use lime on everything. I have heard that lime can be used as a bactericide. I always use it, and therefore, I have never gotten sick from eating the local food. There was only one other table, and it was occupied by a local Mexican family.

We had some time before Marcia would pick us up near the restaurant, so we waited on the white sandy road. When an hour went by, we got bored. There was a family's 20 by 12 feet shack next door to the restaurant near the road, and a Señora was out back cooking dinner on a grill made from a 5 gallon drum using firewood. My dad had an idea that he was going to approach her and ask her in 'sign language' (remember: he speaks zero Spanish) if he could watch her. His communication was successful, and soon we were both watching intently as she prepared handmade corn tortillas from golf ball sized balls of Maseca dough, pressing them down over the fire using pieces of torn paper from the Maseca package in place of pot holders. Through my Spanish, we learned that she was making fish tacos and a large pot of dark green vegetables. We must have attracted the attention of the inhabitants inside the shack because children started coming out to see who was talking with their mother.

There was one child, then another and another and another, all ranging in age from four to eighteen, and the mother's sister, then all of her children also came out of the small shack! Twelve pairs of dark brown eyes stared back at us white gringos. One older daughter spoke a little English and told us that she was going to college in Felipe Carrillo Puerto for a business trade position in technology. As we watched the family go about their daily lives, the mother invited us into their home to eat supper with them. We politely declined since we already ate our meal at the restaurant. Then we exchanged goodbyes and expressed our appreciation for letting us watch her cook. Marcia arrived a little late, but in time for us to make it back to the Mayan Beach Garden Inn to take showers and relax in the bar during the happy hour to chat with guests. We joked with Marcia that she is on Mexican time.

During happy hour and while waiting for our dinner at the inn, my dad and I had piña coladas that were a little too strong. We were drunk silly on one drink each while sitting in the lobby with other guests, laughing to the point of crying. Once we got over our little drunken episode, dinner was served in the screened area connected to the lobby on the beach. I found that I enjoyed the small semi-formal, intimate dinners at the Mayan Beach Garden Inn with all of the guests. There were about 12 of us around one table, and Marcia's husband Kim always joined us. I delighted in listening to his stories about the surrounding area. We learned local slang terms such as square fish and squatters. The phrase square fish is used to denote boxed drug packages washed ashore from Colombia or Venezuela, and squatters is a word used for the locals living on the beach in a shack who do not legally own the land. The setup, hospitality, staff, food, cabañas, and nature and adventure books at the Mayan Beach Garden Inn are outstanding, and Marcia is a wonderful hostess and person.

During one of our days at the inn, I met a naturalist named Jim Conrad. He was staying there for six months in exchange for providing the guests with guided nature walks and Spanish classes, and English classes to the staff. He writes newsletters each week on his website (http://www.backyardnature.net/index.html) about the flora and fauna that he observes at his location. One morning, I went on his beach walk with him before my dad and I continued our plans. Talking as we walked, our attention was suddenly drawn to something laying half in the seawater and half on the beach. It was the oddest creature, and Jim also was curious as to what it was, as he knew it was not found in the Yucatán. It looked like a sea monster out of a science fiction movie or a dead octopus. I thought the mysterious clump was going to start moving, grab us, and swallow us whole like something out of *20,000 Leagues Under the Sea*. The spines looked like tentacles with barbs, and at the base or mouth, there was a clump of fruits that was the size of a basketball. Later, upon the identification by Jim, he told me that my sea monster was actually an African oil palm. The oil palm is native to Africa but recently it has been harvested in Central America, particularly in Honduras. The palm oil is used for making soap and for cooking foods. Since palm oil can tolerate a high temperature, it is good for frying foods: i.e. junk food. Jim and I also observed small slimy sea critters that were in vast quantities all along the shoreline and in the shallow water.

My dad and I had noticed the small pesky creatures while walking the beaches the day before. They bothered me because I knew that I should not walk through them and possibly get them stuck on my legs, especially since I did not know what they were. When in the seawater, they looked exactly like thimbles. After doing some research, we decided that they were probably thimble jellyfish. These marine animals are one inch in diameter and have numerous stinging cells, which can inject poison on contact. Thimble jellyfish are seen in dense clumps along the Mexican Caribbean coast from January to June. Since I am a scientist and curiosity is ingrained in my training, it was refreshing to learn facts, especially when observing the African oil palm, from Jim about the Yucatán coastline that I would have never known otherwise. I found his lifestyle, living simply and cheaply, in exchange for teaching languages, from one interesting place to another, while observing and writing about nature, intriguing and romantic.

When Jim and I finished our morning walk and our discussion about the way he lives, it was time for my dad and me to leave to continue our Punta Herrero section. Our next 15 miles were the hardest of all the 600 miles, but for me, they were the most exciting because of what I saw. The Mayan Beach Garden Inn kitchen staff gave us a ham, lettuce, tomato, and onion sandwich and apple to take with us to eat for lunch on the beach. My dad and I had our picnic lunch in the shade of an old cement lighthouse, which was in ruins. Pelicans stood on the shoreline with watchful eyes.

We knocked off the first few miles easily.

My dad always turned around to see how far we had gone. The lighthouse would soon be a blur as we followed the sandy beach, and each land point would just be like all the other horizons. Our footprints in the sand would also disappear, washed away by the waves.

We could not ignore the unusual winds this year and the 45 mph sustained winds of this particular day made us work harder than ever before.

For one thing, we were walking against the wind, and the gigantic waves and the rough ocean were depositing soft fresh sand on the beach. There was no more hard packed sand to walk on; instead, our feet would sink six inches deep as we trudged along. It was like we were walking in deep snow without snowshoes.

Because of the high winds that blew seawater mist in the air, every five minutes or less, my father had to wipe the salt off his glasses. Everything we wore became caked in salt. The angry ocean hurled a foot and a half long red snapper fish onto the sandy beach. There the fish lay, unable to get back to its home, so my father picked it up and tossed it back in the water. The powerful waves sometimes reached all the way to the edge of the jungle, so there was no beach to walk on; therefore, we found ourselves in waist-high churning seawater. This was dangerous because water logged coconuts, as heavy as bowling bowls, logs sodden with water, and unknown debris smashed against our ankles.

We soon had enough of this brutality and turned to the sandy road for easier and faster travel. The problem with the road was that it would weave around bends, leading us deeper into the jungle and further away from the windswept shoreline. At times, I hated this even more because of the vicious biting quarter-sized flies and other insanity-inducing bugs, lack of a sea breeze to cool us off, and the miserable heat. But the advantage of traveling the jungle road is this: we saw different kinds of animals and plants.

To my surprise and delight, we spotted a five to six foot Central American Boa Constrictor traveling across the hot sandy road. The snake was mild mannered and even let me pet his smooth, beautifully patterned skin before he slithered into the forest and climbed a tree. Witnessing a wild boa constrictor in the jungle made me forget about my nightmares with the biting flies and atrocious heat for the remaining few miles.

The landmark where Marcia was going to pick us up was at the Rancho San Pedro, a few miles north of the Mayan Beach Garden Inn. Walking on the road instead of the beach also made it easier to spot landmarks and the signs of buildings. Rancho San Pedro appeared to be a small private home for renting. There is always a Mexican or Mayan caretaker staying at the place when owners are not present. The Mayan caretaker immediately came to us since he wanted to know why strangers were standing in front of the barbed wire and thick rope surrounding the property. I was not successful at conveying to him, in my simple Spanish, that we wanted to wait here for our ride. But I was able to ask him if we could access the beach through his owner's driveway for a swim. He happily obliged, but he kept us in sight while we cooled our bodies off in the water. The sand on this beach was the softest sand I have ever walked on. I never thought that sand could be this soft. It was like pure velvet.

Upon returning to the road, we stood in front of the Rancho San Pedro sign. The caretaker did not have any water or Cokes for us to buy when we asked, but he gladly opened two coconuts for us to drink. We were not able to communicate very well and we were strangers, however, the caretaker turned out to be accommodating as he even gave us two chairs while we waited for our ride. I was impressed again with the locals' trust and generosity. Finally, Marcia arrived to bring us back to the Inn for dinner and a good night's sleep.

During our coconut-encrusted fish dinner, with the other guests and staff of the inn, we learned important information for our next 20 miles to Majahual. Majahual has a cruise ship dock and is a small tourist town. There could be as many as three ships full of tourists docked at the pier at one time. We learned that there would be two miles of mangroves before Majahual that we would need to get around somehow. There would also be a small river and local fishing community named Rio Indio. Marcia informed us that there is one tiny restaurant in Rio Indio. After exchanging stories about swimming with large boa constrictors in cenotes and exploring remote ruins on the Costa Maya coast, with each of the dinner guests and staff, we excused ourselves for the night.

Upon waking, my legs were so sore from walking in the deep sand the day before that I could barely get out of bed, let alone walk down the stairs from our room. But once we knocked off a couple of miles, the pain went away, as usual. Although once the leg pain went away, carrying the backpack soon became a burden. But it was forgotten when we discovered a pretty jellyfish lying in the sand near the water. It was rare to see such a colorful purple creature along the tropical beaches; the color was almost like a shiny, bright marble. When I learned that it was a Portuguese Man-O-War, it did not seem pretty to me. The stinging cells of a Man-O-War have a neurotoxin and can cause allergic reaction, fever, and anaphylactic shock. The neurotoxin is 75% as powerful as a cobra's venom. Other creatures we noticed were ghost crabs, and they are plentiful along this tropical shoreline, but one should look closely for this animal since you might only see its black eyes. I saw one swimming in the shallow waters and several scampering in the sand. They are called ghost crabs because of the sandy off-white color of their bodies, which help them camouflage within their environment.

We also entertained ourselves by discovering some of nature's other little treasures. We found a water logged palm branch about seven feet long, curved at the end, and a hairy coconut nearby. We pretended these were our Mayan war club and decapitated head. Photos, of course, were taken to make up some exciting but scary tales for the children in Maine. My father was ahead of me, sometimes as much as 500 yards, but that was because I was exploring what was on the ground before me. I was especially interested in a long slithering pattern drawn in the soft sand, several feet away from the water. At first glance, one might think it was a snake, but upon closer observation, I saw foot prints on either side of this *S* shape pattern and knew it had to be a lizard traveling in the sand with its tail dragging.

It was entertaining to see what was around the next beach on this coastline. Thomas Crapper (who, contrary to popular belief, did not invent the toilet, but did help the toilet become popular by inventing the flushing parts to make it more useful) would not be impressed with the makeshift two-seater toilet we saw in the middle of nowhere on the beach. There was no house, camp, or fishermen in the area. The beach outhouse was made out of crude material, mostly trash, and consisted of three and a half corrugated cardboard walls that offered some privacy. Inside, there were two 12 inch holes cut out from plywood for seats and a broken piece of plywood attached to use as a toilet seat cover. It smelled like it was unused. Who made it? My only guess would be fishermen. But I have seen more elaborate outhouses, complete with toilet paper and air fresheners, in the Northern Maine woods! One might wonder if two friends made this and were hoping to share their creation.

Towards the end of the 20 miles for the day, we saw our last marine creature, which is near and dear to my heart. On the shore, partly submerged in the surf, was a large brown log, which was the home of shipworms. For ten years, I conducted research at the University of Maine on shipworms, studying their evolution and symbioses with bacteria. Shipworms are not actually worms, but bivalves as they have two shells connected by a hinge. The common name of shipworms comes from the fact that their body is elongated and they live in and eat wood. Therefore, they destroy wooden ships, lobster traps, and piers. Wood is composed primarily of cellulose matter and is not nutritionally valuable for most animals, but bacteria live in the gut of shipworms and can digest the cellulose by using cellulase enzymes. Shipworms live in all oceans around the world. In the olden days, Caribbean natives used cayenne pepper on the hulls of their wooden boats to prevent shipworm damage. The largest shipworms can be 6.5 feet long, and some shipworms are eaten as delicacies in the Philippines. It was my favorite research project that I conducted at the university.

I said goodbye to my shipworms. We had already walked many miles with our backpacks, and we were starving as it was getting close to the end of the day. We looked for the small fishing community and its restaurant in Rio Indio. By my dad's calculations, we knew it must be coming up. Soon and sure enough, there was a small white building occupied by two señoritas. The sign on the side of the road confirmed that this was indeed the restaurant. Rio Indio was comprised of this restaurant and a few other beach shacks. As we suspected, there was no menu and only the dish of fried fish with all of the usual Mexican fixings was served. This particular plate came with fried plantains, and the fish was extraordinarily tender, moist and delicious.

After the sustainable lunch, Rio Indio was also our place to find a fisherman to boat us across the two miles of mangroves and the small river. This seemed like an easy task, but finding a fisherman turned out to be much more difficult than we could have imagined. There were two boats secured along the shoreline at the Rio Indio community, but at that time, only one elderly man. This man was about the height of a 10 year old, but with excessive wrinkled skin, skinny arms and legs, high cheekbones, and a pointed nose. One boat was a large and heavy dugout canoe and the other was an 18 foot fishing boat with an outboard motor attached. As we pointed to the boat with the motor, I asked in Spanish if we could hire this man to take us across the mangroves so we could continue to walk the beach.

It was not clear if he completely understood me.

When he spoke, I had a hard time understanding what I thought was Spanish. Granted, I did not know the word for mangroves in Spanish, but when he spoke, I did not even understand the word for boat! He walked away, and within seconds he appeared with a long pole in his hands. It appeared that he wanted to take us into the dugout canoe and pole us across the river and swamps. When I attempted to ask Spanish to use the other boat, there was a misunderstanding of language, and we became very frustrated.

My dad and I then found one more man living in a shack near the second boat with a motor. He was our man. We attempted to communicate our needs, and we immediately understood each other. Just to make sure, my dad drew a scenario and map in the sand. When asked how much money he wanted to take us across, the fisherman said, "*Nada*." But we gave him more than enough pesos to cover his gas and time when he dropped us off the beach after the mangroves. As we walked, I thought, *Why did the first old man not understand what we wanted? Why could I not understand him?* I was perplexed and curious, and wondered if he only spoke Mayan.

Later, once in Majahual, I slid up to a bar in the center of town for some pineapple juice. I asked a local bartender, "Is it possible that some old guys don't speak Spanish at all and only speak Mayan?"

He replied, "It is definitely likely as some elderly Mayans don't speak both languages even today."

I felt much better after I learned that miscommunication was not because of my poor Spanish.

After another five to six miles of walking, the outline of a huge orange cruise ship dock in Majahual lay ahead of us on the horizon. We were elated that we had reached the town where we could get all of the cold drinks and food that we wanted, and a place to sleep. We had been walking in 108° F temperatures, full sun, with little drinking water and 20 pound backpacks for about ten hours straight. The effects of the scorching sun had taken its toll on us since we were dehydrated, sun-burnt, and I had a heat rash spreading on my legs.

When we were halfway to the gigantic dock, my dad said, "You look like you are 60 years old!"

I retorted, "I feel like I am *100* years old."

He also mumbled that each year, as we hiked closer to Belize, he felt like he had to add on five years to his life. According to his calculations, that would actually make him 80 years old when we crossed the Belize border.

Images of the cruise ships docked with thousands of tourists in the town of Majahual with its bottomless cold Cokes and beer, bottled water, pineapple juice, Piña Coladas, beef tacos, tortilla chips, fresh fruit, casinos, shopping malls and hammocks kept us pressing on. Unfortunately, our cold drinks, food and hotel were not within our reach. We came to a wall that was about 15 feet high. We attempted to wade through the seawater to the other side, but that proved impossible. My dad started to scale the wall to get to the top, but a security guard came out and starting yelling at us.

Even though I was desperate for something cold to drink, I was so delirious and disappointed and distraught that I could not even think of the word *help* in Spanish. Carrying on a conversation with this unhelpful and rigid security guard was difficult, and the machine gun that he carried over his shoulder was intimidating. I let my dad lead us out of this mess.

I just stood there panicking because there was nothing that the security guard was going to let us do except turn around and go back to where we came from. Of course, that was not an answer my dad was going to accept, so he found a trail that led us through the jungle near the cruise ship dock.

I immediately protested. "But we don't know where this leads. How do you know it's going to take us to Majahual?"

He declared, "It has to lead to the town—it is the only place the trail can go."

I rolled my eyes and sighed.

My dad was right, as usual! Except, another obstacle stood between us and Majahual: a fence that blocked us from getting into what looked like a construction site on the outskirts of town. Luckily, there was a hole that was just big enough for a human to fit through.

Some construction workers with a pickup truck gladly brought us into the center of town. After our fill of drinks and food, we secured a room at La Posada de Los Cañones for between 40.00 and 50.00 USD a night. This inn was marginally satisfactory, but the beach smelled like a sewer. Because of the Great Maya Reef offshore, breaking the waves, there was no wave action onshore, and this caused the water to become stagnant and smelly. Some parts of the seawater were slimy brown; maybe there was a sewer draining into it, or maybe it was just sulfur from rotting vegetation. Either way, this beach was certainly not as lovely as the beaches north of Majahual.

While in our room resting, I laid out my seed and shell collections, which I found during our 100 miles of hiking. I was anxious to admire their beauty, and I marveled at their unique shapes. My favorite trinkets were the sea hearts and hamburger seeds. Sea hearts are the common name for the seeds found in the bean pod of the liana vine (*Genus Entada*). This tropical vine produces the longest bean pod in the world, and the locals call it a monkey ladder. I believe that I have found the perfect sea heart, and it is worth more to me than any amount of money.

I put my collection away before going to bed, and after spending the night at La Posada de Los Cañones, we familiarized ourselves with

Majahual for the day before we continued walking south. We were surprised to discover that 95% of the shops on the ocean front boardwalk were closed and completely void of the usual thousands of tourists whose cruise ships had docked in Majahual. We learned that this was due to the swine flu. The United States travel advisory board had recommended that no cruise ships sail to or dock in Mexico, since the flu pandemic started in Veracruz, Mexico.

From our travels around town, we found another hotel named Matan Ka'an across the dirt street. We liked the clean refreshing indoor pool, extensive colorful hotel décor, friendly staff, and it was only an extra 10.00 USD a night, so we decided to switch hotels.

I found the Telavera sinks in the Costa Maya area gorgeous.

One will see these sinks at the Mayan Beach Garden Inn and at Matan Ka'an. Talavera is handmade ceramic pottery from the state of Puebla. The colors of the sink in one of the public bathrooms in the lobby of Matan Ka'an were greens, yellow, white, and black; and the other bathroom sink was rusty, orange, green and black. The bathroom in our new room was luxuriously colorful with reds, oranges, and yellows on the sink, counter, light fixtures, the soap and toothbrush holders, and the mirror; all of them matched with the same pattern. I have always loved bright and cheerful colors. Even the shower was interesting in that the front shower wall had a hole near the top, and its shape reminded me of the hole that was used during the ancient Mayan Pok-a-Tok ball game.

All of these exquisite decorations contrasted with the six inch land crab in my bedroom trying to hide squished between the wall and desk leg. It reminded me of a huge mutated spider. A freakin' gigantic crab with eight legs did not belong in my room!

I yelled to my dad, "Get this thing out of here!"

My dad caught the creepy, ugly crab in his baseball hat and placed it outside.

Once we had a restful night at Matan Ka'an, our goal for the next day was to keep walking south to Punta Kanecaxh (pronounced Kan-e-cash, as the x in Mayan is usually pronounced as "sh") for one more entire day, using this hotel as our base. It is easier doing our daily walking without having to carry our backpacks. We looked forward to any portion of our walks where we did not have to carry our belongings. We figured this time we would hitchhike back to the Majahual hotel at the end of the day.

There were many adventures waiting for us during the next 20 miles. They included an eight inch cushion starfish living on driftwood during low tide that looked like a pin cushion; a cute brown, white and black dog that became my friend and companion for two hours; neon colored buildings; a lone lime-green boat anchored at sea; another boat that was partially submerged upside down in the waves; total destruction of a resort from Hurricane Dean; and a lot of burnt skin from the hot sun.

But my two favorite memories while walking from Majahual to Punta Kanecaxh for the day were, first, the plastic tables and chairs underneath the sea grape trees, situated on the beach in front of a small stucco house, which gave me immediate images of jolly fat Mexican men playing dominoes while smoking Cuban cigars. Second, near the end of day, when we were getting thirsty and since I did not have my machete, I wanted to find a native with a tool to open a coconut for drinking. Luck had it that there was a uniformed Mexican patrolling the beach with a machete, and when I presented him with a wild coconut, he hacked off the end, leaving a hole that contained the coconut water.

The coconut water did not satisfy our thirst, so when we stumbled upon a beach hotel bar around 5:00 pm, we took advantage of their hospitality and trudged up the soft hot sand to the bar for cold pineapple and mango juice. The hotel's name was El Castillo (which means *the castle* in English), and the bar was the home of a brown and white spider, with a three inch long body that lived in his web over the bartender's head. The spider first appeared to be fake, but, upon questioning the bartender who flicked its web, the spider showed me that it was indeed alive. When ready to hitchhike back to Majahual, we snuck our way to the road using someone's property through a barbed wire fence. Hitchhiking in Mexico is still practiced, and from my experiences in the Yucatán, safe. I have even taken turns with my dad sticking my thumb out while standing on the side of the dirt beach roads.

This ends our hike for this year, but certainly not our adventures for our remaining couple of days in Mexico. On our last day in Majahual, while waiting for Luis to pick us up and take us to Felipe Carrillo Puerto, I wanted to find a señorita or señora to braid my hair island-girl style. I found a lady that owned a little boutique that would do it for a total of 15.00 USD. It is worth mentioning that, two days later, as we traveled towards Cancún because the day of our flight was near, I asked the staff at Iberostar Lindo in Mayan Riviera how much they would charge for the same exact braids. The Mexican lady told me 70.00 USD!

One of my favorite stops along the long jungle road to Felipe Carrillo Puerto was in Limones because there were roadside farmers' stands with bountiful fruits and fresh vegetables. Luis stopped at one, and we purchased two types of juicy sweet mangos, pineapple, cucumbers, and oranges. Back in Felipe Carrillo Puerto, we were happy to have made friends like Luis and his family to show us places near and in the city that we would have never known of venturing to by ourselves.

Traveling towards Cancún at the end of the week, the bus dropped us off in Playa del Carmen around noon after we traveled from Carrillo Puerto for three hours. My father wanted to mingle with other Americans and Europeans, and eat American food at a resort the last two nights before our flight, so I went along with this plan. Dad swore that he knew the location of an Iberostar resort in Playa del Carmen.

So, he suggested we walk with our backpacks as it would only take "a few minutes."

A few minutes turned into what seemed like a few hours as he could not find Iberostar. We ended up walking aimlessly around Playa del Carmen looking for an all-inclusive resort that would either allow us to stay for only two nights in our filthy, smelly condition that was not outrageously expensive or one that was open! It turned out that most resorts were also closed because of the travel advisory recommended by the State Department due to the swine flu endemic. Without anything to eat in six hours and no water to drink, we walked over two miles, in the hottest part of the day, in the tourist city with our belongings. Except, I could no longer carry my backpack because I felt like I was going to pass out! So, my superhuman father decided that he could carry two backpacks for half of the search.

We finally walked into the classy Sandos All-Inclusive Beach Resort and sat down in the fancy lobby's plush white oversized chairs. We got curious stares from the rich sophisticated tourists. The hotel staff certainly was not going to give us vagabonds a room for two nights. But my father was experienced enough that he knew, if he pretended to act like he belonged there, the hotel concierge would give us complimentary glasses of juice. The juice hit the spot, and after we talked the hotel staff into letting us pay for only two nights, we decided that it was too expensive anyway, and we took a collectivo along Highway 307 to the Mayan Riviera Iberostar Lindo, which was open and cheaper.

My dad was content now that he could speak English with fellow Americans and eat familiar food. But I was not, and I wanted to test my new skills while being a foreign female traveler *without* my dad to help me. After spending one night at Iberostar, I realized that I needed to immerse myself in the Mexican culture and could do it by spending less than 20.00 USD. I had enough time before our flight the next day to go back to Felipe Carrillo Puerto, so I decided to take the leap and venture off by myself for the afternoon and evening. I told my dad that I would return to the resort that night.

Arriving at Playa del Carmen's ADO bus station, I confidently walked to the ticket window and in Spanish asked for a one way ticket, which was 7.00 USD. The three hour ride was long, but I occupied myself by reading one of the trashy novels left at Iberostar by the numerous tourists, looking out the window at the Yucatán jungle, and pleasing all my senses with the activity from the local Mayan Indian passengers, mostly families. Once in my beloved Mayan city, I knew that I could call on Luis and his family to help me get around.

So, that is what I did, and I had an interesting barbecue fish taco dinner cooked on the family's homemade grill in the deep pueblos on a back dirt road. I felt very fortunate to practice my Spanish and experience

Mexican life this way. Everything was going as planned, and I felt very safe. But I did not want to miss my bus ride back or have my dad worry about me. I arrived at the Carrillo Puerto bus station at 7:30 pm to take the 8:30 pm bus back to Playa del Carmen.

That was when things started going amiss.

When 8:30 pm arrived and I had purchased my ticket to Playa del Carmen, there was no bus with a destination of Playa del Carmen parked outside. The station attendants clearly stated that the buses currently parked at the station were not going to Playa del Carmen. Another hour went by, and I started to wonder if I did not understand their Spanish and whether I had missed the bus. It is sometimes difficult to understand the local dialect from uneducated natives. It was a good thing that I do not panic easily. I stayed calm and waited. Besides, I had nowhere to go, and my flight home was about 12 hours away. However, my dad was expecting me back in our fancy resort room. During that waiting time, every half hour, I would find a station attendant, show him my Playa del Carmen ticket, and he would rigorously nod his head while saying, "Sí, el autobús no está aquí todavia."

I waited alone for two more hours until the bus finally pulled up at 11:30 pm.

This was when it *really* got interesting. I boarded the bus with the Mayan passengers and took a seat directly in the front across from the bus driver's seat. Several minutes passed as we sat there waiting, and the bus driver still had not entered the bus and taken his seat. I had a feeling that something else was wrong. Soon, I found out. Every time the engine of the bus was started, the electrical system would go haywire—the head lights and air conditioner would turn off, the radio would turn on, the lights on the dash would flicker, turn signals would blink, and the wipers would move. This whole bizarre performance was just like Christine, the 1958 Plymouth Fury from the movie in which she is the titular antagonist.

When four Mexicans lifted the hood of the bus in the front, I looked forward. Watching them closely, I could see that they were attempting to fix it with tape and string! This is no joke. They were literally jerry-rigging it with rudimentary parts and supplies. When the driver started the engine this time, everything worked perfectly. This was apparently satisfactory to all expert mechanics involved, so we departed towards the dark Yucatán jungle at midnight on a lonely road for three hours. The other passengers were not aware of any of this; they had already fallen asleep as soon as they had boarded the bus.

So here I was, a lone 41-year-old female gringa who speaks no Mayan and little Spanish, who could not understand a word of their elementary backwoods Spanish, on a dilapidated bus, which has been repaired with office supplies, traveling through the stifling jungle in the wee hours of the night. My only worry was that I needed to stay awake, otherwise, I would end up on the other side of the Yucatán peninsula in Mérida. To accomplish this, I munched on oatmeal cookies and pumpkin seeds, and washed it down with iced tea that I picked up at the bus station. I also watched the bus driver to make sure he was not falling asleep as he kept yawning. I noticed that, as two to three buses passed us, he would shine his lit up cell phone through the large windshield, moving it up and down quickly to signal to the other driver. His signal would be returned in the same fashion. It was like a secret coded light that the bus drivers shared. To keep him awake, I shared my cookies with him. He seemed to appreciate that very much. Through my simple Spanish conversations, he knew that I was trying to stay awake and keep him from falling asleep.

I arrived in Playa del Carmen with no incidents, although it was 2:00 am, and finally pulled up to the Iberostar gate in the Mayan Riviera by taxi. I stated my name and room number to the gate security.

Suddenly, security guards with machine guns swarmed the taxi. "Ma'am, please step out of the car." I obeyed their order, and then they fired off questions in English.

"What is your name? Your room number? Are you hurt?"

I responded to each question.

"Where have you been? Why are you returning so late?"

I answered meekly, "I was in Felipe Carrillo Puerto for the afternoon and evening, and the bus back to Playa del Carmen was three hours late."

Then the name Richard Bailey came up.

The security guards explained that my father had reported me missing!

That is what dads are for, I suppose, worrying about their daughters even when they are over 40 years of age. I quickly explained to my Dad that the bus was three hours late, and it arrived broken-down. I think my Dad felt more at ease that I returned safely, although maybe not impressed at the hour. Just the act of getting to and from Felipe Carrillo Puerto on my own was an exciting adventure for me.

Even though the guidebooks pass Carrillo Puerto off as nothing to do for tourists in this area, my Dad and I found plenty of noteworthy excursions on the few occasions that we have visited. I have a feeling that no other tourists have been to some of these places. I really enjoyed immersing myself in a different culture and visiting places that only locals know about, especially local swimming pools, cenotes, and events held in the center park.

CHAPTER 8

Felipe Carrillo Puerto and the Interview with a Local Mayan

• • •

DURING THE WINTER OF 2009, I read about the Mayan city Felipe Carrillo Puerto, and I discovered that the city is named after a famous governor of the Yucatán state.

Felipe Carrillo Puerto was elected governor of the Yucatán state in 1922, and he was a descendent of the last Mayan king who fought against the Spanish. The elected governor was popular because he believed in equal rights for women and the indigenous Mayan communities. He has been called "the Abraham Lincoln of Mexico."

Back in the United States, a San Francisco reporter named Alma Reed made a name for herself by supporting poor Mexicans and human rights. She wrote a newspaper column and gave legal advice to people who could not afford a lawyer, and many of those people were poor Mexicans who lived in California. Reed received a letter from a family with a young son who sat on death row. He had been sentenced to death after his state-appointed lawyer suggested, in incomprehensible English, that he plead guilty. Reed defended the 17-year-old Mexican non-English-speaking migrant worker in California. Her campaign was successful, and the young boy's life was saved. As a result of her efforts, the California legislature passed an amendment in 1921 that prohibited the execution of a minor. In addition, officials in Mexico recognized Reed. She was invited to visit the current President of Mexico in Mexico City.

Months later, as a journalist who wanted to return to Mexico, she embarked on an expedition to the Yucatán, funded by Carnegie Expedition, to cover the excavation of the ruins Chichén Itzá by archaeologists. Upon stepping off the train, she heard a Mariachi band singing a welcoming song, "Alma de mi Alma." Thinking that it was for her, she started crying. Little did she know, it was not for her, but for a businessman.

It was during this trip that Alma Reed and Felipe Carrillo Puerto met, fell in love at first sight, and became engaged. She thought of him as a Greek deity, and he called her Almita. When the Governor heard about the song at the train station and Alma's emotional reaction, he wrote a love ballad for her called "La Peregrina," which means The Pilgrim. However, eleven days before their planned wedding, Carrillo Puerto was shot to death by his enemies. Before the order of assassination was given, he requested that the Mayan wedding ring in his pocket be given to his fiancé.

Reed continued her work in Mexico, focusing on art, journalism, and archaeology. She was awarded the "Order of the Aztec Eagle," which is the highest decorated medal given to foreigners in Mexico. In 1966, Reed died of cancer, and the manuscript of her autobiography was lost. However, in 2001, the dusty autobiography was discovered by Michael K. Schuessler in an empty apartment in Mexico City.

The story fascinated me, and I could not wait to arrive in Carrillo Puerto to experience the Mayan city firsthand, especially since it was off the beaten path and rich with Mayan culture. This chapter will describe some of the adventures that are not associated with the actual walking from Cancún to Belize. It will also include the interview that I conducted to learn about this city through the eyes of a local.

Each year, from 2009 to 2011, when we returned to Carrillo Puerto, we reserved 3 to 4 extra days to join in local excursions before continuing our coastal hike. Every time we arrived, we found our friend Luis to hire and we spent some time with the locals.

My father and I came back to Carrillo Puerto after hiking for the week in 2009 and stayed in our favorite hotel, Chan Santa Cruz, which is right across from the central park. During our first night, while strolling in the park, the locals prepared for a children's show in the culture house, La Casa Cultura. We were invited as guests of Luis and Xally at no charge.

It was one of the most memorable and privileged experiences for my dad and me because, even though we were outsiders in this Mayan city, we were taken in as guests of family and shared their experiences. The evening show took place in the outdoor stage area, underneath the stars in the humid jungle air, and we took our seats while surrounded by Mayans. The hot tropical sun disappeared into the forest, off in the distance, casting its shadows over the old stucco buildings in the park. We were the only gringos in the entire culture house. The show was intended for young children since it consisted of silly friendly clowns performing funny tricks and young Mayan girls dancing in their traditional colorful dresses, spurred on by ancient tribal music. Each girl wore a white blouse and their skirts were bright blue, pink, red, purple or gold. One girl in the middle was the tallest, and her pretty lipstick stood out against on her smooth dark skin, jet black hair, and beautiful eyes, and she styled her hair with a crimson flower. Back in our hotel room that night, I reflected on how fortunate we were to witness and share that special family event in La Casa Cultura.

That next morning, I woke up to church bells ringing from the park across the street.

For our plans that day, my father suggested finding a swimming pool to cool off.

After calling Luis and Juan, I was able to communicate our plans to Juan who spoke better English. They thought it was a great idea and we all met up again with our bathing suits. My dad and I were pleasantly surprised about 20 miles later, on the outskirts of the city, when we arrived at this local swimming pool that is fed by a natural cenote and family-owned by a former Mayan guide. I believe that the name of the property is Familia de Los Ék. The owner had an elderly father who dreamed about providing a place for the local kids to cool off. This clean refreshing pool was surrounded the lush Yucatán jungle. And the guide spoke perfect English.

I was immediately impressed and delighted by this whole set-up. It appeared that they were still building this property, and I wished that someday I could volunteer at a place like this and assist in setting up and maintaining it; I even had dreams of going into the guiding business with the former Mayan guide. The father and son also served us cold Cokes and coconut water, freshly cut from the palm trees in the jungle, for a dollar. I will never forget what the former guide said as my dad told him our story. While I was swimming in the pool, the five guys told stories and laughed it up underneath the palapa while drinking Cokes and cocowater. Now that my dad had a translator, there was quite a stir among the Mexican locals regarding our walk from Cancún to Belize. I do not think that the guide believed my father; so, he proceeded to get confirmation by asking me.

The English speaking guide marched over to me with a baffled look on his face and proclaimed, "There seems to be some misunderstanding. I thought your father said you walked from Cancún to Majahaul. That is impossible!"

After a swim in the cool, fresh cenote water, we left this wonderful gem in the Yucatán jungle with the father and son who had impressions of my father and me as either great adventurers or crazy gringos. I hope to someday pass through there again.

Our next adventure was during the same day in the afternoon. Upon leaving Luis and Juan, my father suggested that we find a cenote in the jungle. We would just wave down any taxi driver and ask him to take us to a cenote. How difficult could it be to use Spanish to convey this wish? We found a taxi, and the driver zipped us through the busy, colorful, stucco-lined streets of Carrillo Puerto. He brought us to the outskirts and had us walk in the jungle for several yards on a trail. We ended up at the edge of a muddy, swampy, bug-infested, hot lake. The word for lake or lagoon in Spanish is *laguna*.

We repeatedly said, "No, *cenote*, por favor."

The Mayan would nod vigorously, stretch out his arms toward the lake, and say "Si, cenote."

We never found our typical remote sinkhole in the forest that day, although the Yucatán is reported to be dotted with thousands of them. My guess is that these lakes in the middle of the forest are freshwater sinkholes and therefore are also called cenotes by the Mayans. Or the taxi driver just wanted to make money.

However, we did not give up our quest to find a true mystical cenote, hidden away in a remote area. So, the next day, we called on our newly found friends, Luis and Juan. Of course, they delivered us to a cenote with adventurous spirit and a story.

Not too far from the center of Felipe Carrillo, Juan drove us to the edge of the jungle and we all got out of the car to walk on a trail for about 20 minutes. While walking, I thought to myself, "How many tourists have been on this trail without a true guide?"

The Yucatán forest then opened up to the most beautiful remote cenote, descending about 30 feet below the surface and about 70 feet in diameter. I have never seen a more magical geological setting in my life. Luis told me that the cenote was named Azul De X-Pichil. Azul De X-Pichil had multiple twisted vines hanging from the surface of the earth down to its cool refreshing water. Various creatures, such as poisonous snakes, spiders, scorpions, and bats, probably lived within its crevices.

Being in the humid sticky jungle and sweating profusely, my dad and I wanted to jump into the fresh cold water, but thought twice when we wondered how we would return to the surface. We could climb back up using the vines, but it was too far, he was too old, and I was not strong enough. The vines were too twisted, as well, and did not make a clear path to the top, and creatures lived behind these vines. Our dilemma was solved when Juan offered to drive back to the nearest pueblo to look for a rope. He left us alone in the forest with Luis for almost an hour.

While my dad and I were standing on the edge of the 30 foot deep sink hole, wishing we could jump in, my mind started to wander. I thought, "How did we know that Luis didn't have a gun or knife and planned on robbing us and pushing us over?" We have all heard of the recent increase in drug related horrific crime in Mexico. Your senses become more in tuned and magnified when traveling, especially when it comes to safety. Nobody knew where my dad and I were at that moment. Luis was a stranger that we had only met a few days before.

Then, the funniest thing happened. Juan returned with a rope, but it was only ½ inch thick! Who can climb up a rope of that thickness? Disappointed, we politely declined his offer after waiting. But Luis jumped in and being much younger, he was able to climb out using the rope and twisted roots.

Of course, it turned out that nothing bad happened to my dad and I, and Luis became our trusted friend over the three years of visiting Felipe Carrillo Puerto. I eventually learned to think of him as a protector, almost like a brother.

The next year, 2010, was the year that we crossed the Belize border, which meant that, although we would pass through Carrillo Puerto and needed Luis to bring us to the coast to start walking, we did not return to the Mayan City at the end of that week to spend time exploring.

However, in the following year of 2011, we returned for more exploration and to conduct the interviews. We looked for a hotel named La Ceiba with a swimming pool, La Capilla, which means "the chapel" in English, according to the internet. We walked for miles at 9:30 pm, on back streets of Carrillo Puerto, after traveling for 18 hours to get there with our backpacks and without food or water to find La Ceiba. When asking locals on the street, they had never heard of it. I also had a post-broken arm from skiing over that winter with my arm still in a removable cast. The hotel turned out to be on the outskirts of town, far away, on the opposite end from my beloved park. It was a simple hotel for about 45.00 USD a night, and I thought that the Chan Santa Cruz Hotel was slightly more appealing because it was closer to the center of town, the markets, the restaurants, and the park. But our main attraction to La Ceiba was the large pools and the staff members who were considerably more personable, as well as the owner, who was the uncle of the local Mayan that I would interview.

My dad and I went to bed that night with no lunch or dinner, but we did persuade the nighttime caretaker of the hotel to sell us some water to drink. I awoke that morning feeling refreshed; there is nothing better than waking up in the tropics after a night of sweet-smelling humidity lulling you to sleep with the humming of a ceiling fan to cool your sticky skin. My dad and I walked to the center of town for breakfast, this time in the daylight.

Since this was our third time visiting this Mayan City, I felt at home and wanted to be very adventurous and try breakfast at the public outdoor market with the Mexicans and Mayans. The market had long tables covered in red cloth, and in a row on the tables, there were small coolers with different flavored empanadas for sale. The choices, written in marker and Spanish, were potato and cheese, sausage and cheese, ham and cheese, or mushroom and cheese with a variety of flavorful sauces to choose from. There were also fresh tropical fruit stands and drinks. We chose one each of ham and cheese, and potato and cheese empanadas, a fruit plate and our drinks. The cost for one meal was 1.80 USD. We were the only Americans at the market.

My dad, of course, was not so adventurous with the food, but went along with my idea of eating at the market anyway. In fact, he kept complaining that day was Easter, and at home, our family was probably eating a New England Easter dinner that consisted of baked ham, scalloped potatoes, and apple pie. Every time he would pose smiling for a picture, he would joke that he would not be smiling when he was sick because of the market food. But that never happened. I enjoyed our adventurous and cheap breakfast, and would eat there again without hesitation. After our meal, we walked through the rest of the outdoor farmer's market, where the vendors sold everything from beans, garlic, tropical fruit, variety of colorful ripe peppers, and raw fly-covered meat dripping with blood on the street.

After breakfast, we walked towards the park on our way to find Juan's and Luis's house. I knew it was near the park, and I remembered which street number the house was on. Along the way, my dad spotted a young boy dribbling a basketball in the street. They started passing the ball to each other. My dad thoroughly enjoyed teaching this young Mayan the moves of a basketball player, dribbling behind his back and through his legs, basically showing off. Since my dad towers over every Mayan and Mexican at six feet, and since we were the only white people in the town, he could only think that the boy would return to his mother later that day and exclaim, "Mom, I saw an NBA basketball player from the United States in the street, and he showed me some moves!"

I laughed at the NBA incident as we continued walking towards Juan's and Luis's house. We found the house, and Juan's wife came out to greet us, inviting my dad and me to wait in the house until the guys showed up. She also offered us some refreshing orange Tang drinks. Within minutes, Juan's teenage daughter Giselle came out to sit with us. She was polite, sociable, and friendly. She seemed fascinated by my pictures, about Maine, my dog, and my dad, and about our walk to Central America. She was also curious about my broken wrist. I was pleased to practice my Spanish, and she spoke some English. I enjoyed interacting with children in Mexico.

When Luis and Juan, arrived they asked us if we wanted to go kayaking with them.

Giselle joined us.

We drove in Juan's taxi for about 30 minutes to a lagoon visited only by local families, stopping along the way to pick up a whole roasted chicken, homemade salsa in tied bags, fresh tortillas, cabbage and beer for a picnic by the lagoon. It was a beautiful sandy beach with crystal clear water fed by a cenote. The weather, although windy, was sunny and warm. We ate chicken tacos on the picnic tables, then rented kayaks and rowed along the shore. We did not see any animals, but rowed upon some children swinging on a rope from the shore out into the deep water. We didn't stay out long because of the wind and I wasn't able to paddle because of my post-broken wrist.

We spent the rest of the afternoon swimming in the lagoon, splashing, and laughing even though we couldn't understand a word of each other's languages. Unfortunately, most of these local places are so off the beaten path that they did not have a name or the language barrier was such a problem that I was unable to get the names or the history of these places.

I spent the rest of my days in Felipe Carrillo Puerto locating and interviewing a local public school director and Mayan named José edier

Yama. José was a top student of Catherine Gray who is an English teacher in Felipe Carrillo, and she is married to Luis's daughter's uncle. We met Catherine in the park one year during our visit to Felipe Carrillo. She set up the interview for me. José is also an elementary school teacher in Felipe Carrillo and was born in 1961 in Señor, Quintana Roo, a small pueblo outside of Felipe Carrillo Puerto. He has lived in Carrillo Puerto all of his life and is 100% Mayan. Since this was my first interview, and I have no training in journalism, I was very nervous. But José made me feel comfortable and was professional.

Upon setting up a meeting place and time, I met José and he led me to the Mayan Ceremonial Center, the sanctuary for the talking cross and sacred temple. The site was definitely off the beaten path, as I would have never found it on my own, and I would have felt uncomfortable walking in without my Mayan guide because some of the locals do not like tourists in the Ceremonial Center. The guard, who stood watch 24 hours a day at the entrance, asked me to remove my shoes, hat, and take no pictures.

The Center played an important part in the 1847 War of the Castes, which started when the native Mayans revolted against the population of European descent. The legend claims that, when the Mayans were defeated in Valladolid and Merída, they fled to the jungle to build a secret city called Chan Santa Cruz (small holy cross), now known as Felipe Carrillo Puerto. FCP was founded in 1850. The Mayans carved a cross on a mahogany tree to mark the area. The cross mimicked the voice of God and instructed the Mayans to keep fighting. However, the talking cross was actually a priest and ventriloquist hired by the rebel leader José Maria Barrera. Even though the Mayans were tired of struggling, the cross enabled the Mayans to gain confidence. The Mexican government was stunned when they found this secret city with a population of 10,000 Indians. The center is set on a rocky slope with a cenote that also served as fresh drinking water and refuge for the Mayan rebels. The Indians kept fighting until 1915 when the Mexican government declared Quintana Roo an independent state.

After the Ceremonial Center tour, José took me to the park in the center of town. We sat on the benches, and he answered some questions about the city of Felipe Carrillo Puerto and his life.

"What do you think of the changes, both ancient and new, that the governor of the Yucatán state has made in the Mayan communities?" I asked.

He answered, "That communication and organization have improved. And today, the crime rate is low in Felipe Carrillo Puerto, but alcoholism is prevalent."

I also found the Mayan dresses beautiful, so I wanted to know more about them. Women's original Yucatecan huipil embroidered dresses are worn only by older women in FCP, but if one goes out into the smaller surrounding pueblos, all women wear the traditional dress. The Mayan dress is like a loose-fitting tunic made from pieces of fabric which are joined together by stitching, ribbons or other fabric pieces, and heavily decorated. These dresses are much more elaborate and old-fashioned than the skirts and white blouses worn by the children in the Cultural House show.

José seemed appreciative that I was asking about his life and town, so I kept on asking questions. "Do the children in Carrillo Puerto formally learn about the governor in school?"

José answered, "They do not learn about him, but I learned about him from my elementary art teacher."

On a positive note, he told me that 40% of the population speaks Mayan and the language is still taught in school. To learn more about the ancient people, artifacts, and history, one can visit the Tihosuco museum in a village that dates back to 1534 and is located near Carrillo Puerto.

When asked about the culinary cuisine in Carrillo Puerto, José taught me the names of the popular dishes like salbutes. Salbutes are crispy corn tortillas topped with shredded turkey, avocado, pickled onions and cabbage. I ate my first three salbutes while on the local bus back to Playa del Carmen. The Mayan ladies in their traditional dress were standing at the bus station curb, balancing a large platter of them over their heads, selling them for a peso each.

The other well-known foods in Carrillo Puerto are chirmole (Guatemalan tomato sauce), beans with chili and corn, and panuchos. Panuchos are similar to salbutes, but the tortilla is cooked until it is puffy then stuffed with refried beans and lightly fried so the inside has a creamy texture. Jose also explained to me that, in the old days, his ancestors ate animals in the jungle that were much more delicious. I cannot imagine the food being tastier than salbutes and panuchos.

I learned of four festivals that are popular in this Mayan City from José. They are Three Kings, which happens on January 6th, Carnival Festival, which happens in February, La Cruz, which happens on May 3rd, and Guadeloupe, which happens on December 12th. January sixth is when the three kings, or wise men, brought gifts to baby Jesus. Traditionally, some children in Mexico receive gifts on the sixth of January, instead of Christmas, December 25th, which they consider an imported custom. Mexicans also celebrate Three Kings religious activities, bullfighting, and traditional dances.

In February, city officials in Carrillo Puerto organize Carnival Celebration in the main park. Carnival is full of street parades, street parties and festivals with the purpose of getting all the craziness out of people's lives before Easter. May 3rd is the celebration of the Holy Cross (La Cruz), which bricklayers and members of the construction industry celebrate by putting a cross on a building they constructed.

Finally, on December 12th, the country of Mexico celebrates the Lady of Guadalupe; this is the most popular and traditional festival in Mexico. This holiday is only celebrated by Catholics since the Lady of Guadalupe is the Roman Catholic icon of Virgin Mary. Many pilgrims run or bike from towns or cities, carrying torchlights because they usually travel at night to protect them from the sun. Pilgrims sing Las Mañanitas to the Guadalupe Virgin and the priest holds a mass.

I also asked José, "How do the locals feel about tourists visiting Carrillo Puerto? Every time my dad and I visit this city, I see maybe one other tourist."

José confirmed, "About five to six tourists visit a month, although I would like to see more."

In my opinion, I would like to see the cultural center of Carrillo Puerto untouched by Americans and Europeans since I have seen the effects of tourism in Cancún and Playa del Carmen. I only saw American influences in Carrillo Puerto one day, in the form of music and snacks at our local hotel pool, La Capilla. The music blasting from the speakers was performed by the popular American groups such as the Black Eyed Peas and the Village People, who sang YMCA in the middle of the Yucatán jungle. The best lunch I have ever had was at this pool—little slices of American hotdogs simmered in hot sauce, Mexican style, accompanied by cubes of mango and cucumber, all to be eaten with toothpicks. I learned from José that the best time to visit Carrillo Puerto was between April and September because Mayans like it hot.

At the end of the interview and on our way back to my hotel, I mentioned that one of my favorite foods is tamales and asked where to find some. José explained that his mother just made some for the Easter celebration, and while I waited in the outdoor hotel lobby, he returned with some delicious chicken tamales that I ate for lunch. In addition, José's uncle, who was also the owner of the hotel where my dad and I were staying, opened up his car trunk where there were fresh ripe mangoes just picked from his yard. Chicken tamales and mangoes made a great refreshing lunch on a hot Mexican day!

I thanked José and his uncle for their hospitality, and we all posed for pictures to remember our time in Felipe Carrillo Puerto with our friends.

My last evening and day in Mexico were also quite memorable. My dad wanted to eat his final dinner at the park restaurant that serves ham sandwiches and French fries. But I wanted a little more spice and culture in my meal, so I set off by myself, looking for the perfect Mexican dinner: chile rellenos and a banana smoothie. I even ate my dinner while watching a sports game on TV. The Mexico City Club América team was playing fútbol or soccer.

Chile rellenos are roasted poblano chile peppers stuffed with cheese, then fried. They were most delicious smothered with homemade tomato salsa at the restaurant I found named El Faisán y El Venado, "The

Pheasant and The Deer." At the end of my evening, while walking back towards our hotel, I searched in the small local clothing shops along the streets for an authentic Club América soccer jersey. I found one that was only 10.00 USD, which would have been 70.00 USD online in the United States. I only paid 10.00 USD, and I made an adventure out of practicing my Spanish with the local señorita employee who helped me find this jersey. That was a lot more fun than sitting at a computer ordering online.

Early in the morning, on our last full day in Mexico, I met with Catherine Gray at her house in Felipe Carrillo Puerto, and she took me to her Culture and Language Institute, Na'atik. The Mayan word Na'atik translates into "understanding," and the Institute's mission is to provide high quality language courses in Mayan, Spanish, English, and French, in a fun and cultural environment, to foreigners and locals. The Institute also engages in active fieldtrips to the surrounding Mayan Mexican communities. This kind of language school is much needed in Felipe Carrillo Puerto.

Its website is http://www.naatikmexico.com/.

Catherine is originally from Virginia in the United States, and she did some volunteering in Felipe Carrillo Puerto years ago. While visiting Carrillo Puerto, she fell in love with a local Mexican Mayan named Pedro, and he is her husband who also founded Na'atik. I was impressed with the beginnings of the Institute since they were just completing the building and did not have students yet.

As I said goodbye to Felipe Carrillo Puerto, Cancún, and Mexico this year, I hoped that someday I would return not only as an adventurer but also as a volunteer at Na'atik or at the local swimming pool that my dad and I visited, Familia de Los Ék.

CHAPTER 9

Punta Kanecaxh, Mexico to Belize: My National Geographic Moment

• • •

THIS WAS A MOMENTOUS 120 mile section for us because we crossed the Belize border and ended our journey. In 2010, we traveled from Punta Kanecaxh to XCalak, the end of Quintana Roo, then onto Cay Ambergris, Belize. We would then walk the beaches of Cay Ambergris, from north to south, to San Pedro. We received a lot of publicity with this adventure, including a website, a fundraiser for cancer research, Maine state-wide presentations, several local and national interviews, and international articles.

My winter research notes from *The Lost World of Quintana Roo* revealed that Peissel sailed from Rio Indio to XCalak, stopping over in XCalak before sailing to British Honduras. He did not walk this section from Rio Indio to XCalak. And, probably the most alarming note that I made was that, once Peissel had crossed the border, he was thrown in the Belizean jail! The police explained to Peissel that travelers were required to have a visa to enter Belize, and no one was allowed to enter through San Pedro. In other words, they told him to go back to where he came from because he "crashed the border." The officials did not believe for a second that he had just walked 200 miles from Mexico to Belize, even with his blackened skin from sun exposure, tattered sandals, and a moldy backpack.

Were we not entering the same way just fifty years later?

Although, you do not need a visa anymore, normal tourists enter Belize by a cruise ship, flying into San Pedro or Belize City, or by car, and check in at the proper border crossings. I wrote to all embassies and consulates to make sure we could get in legally. My other immediate concern was the fact that the section from Punta Kanechaxh to XCalak would be the most remote area that we would hike. From the topographical map, online searches, and my other inquiries, I knew there were absolutely no pueblos with drinking water on this stretch of the coast, only a river and possibly a small resort.

Crossing a river would be another problem. The river Rio Huach runs along the Yucatán coast between Mahahual and XCalak. On www.locogringo.com, aerial photos showed a bridge, but images on Google Earth showed no bridge. They claimed that the bridge burnt down in 2006, and no one replaced it! The nearest settlement was about six miles north of Rio Huach.

I called my dad in a panic, saying, "How are we going to get across this river?"

He said, "Don't worry. I can get us over it. The last time we needed to get over an inlet during this hike, I made a raft, remember?"

One website told me that Rio Huach had crocodiles in it, but another site told me that the river was safe to swim in! I had secretly wished to see a crocodile. I was also told that on the other side of this river there was hotel property. I thought we could wait on the north side of this river and wave to a fisherman or a guide with a boat to take us across. It sounded like I would be coming home with yet another story of how we triumphed over more obstacles.

Fortunately, I found the hotel Costa de Cocos, located in XCalak, online, and because of the publicity of this walk, I became acquainted with the owner, Ilana Randall. Through emails, I made deals to have the hotel staff arrange a trip with a captain and harbor master from XCalak to get our border crossing paperwork and hire a boat for the crossing. I also found out from Costa de Cocos that the bridge over Rio Huach actually burnt down in 2003. This, of course, left no way to get to XCalak by vehicle from Majahual, unless we drove all the way around to Chetumal.

So, off we went with our research notes, trustworthy backpacks, machete, bottles of water and trail mix in the spring of 2010 to conquer this last stretch of the Mayan Coast, Quintana Roo. I had mixed emotions, excitement and sadness that this might be my last big adventure with my dad, since, when we crossed into Belize, we would complete our goal.

To get to the southern coast, the only road was through Felipe Carrillo Puerto. We stayed in the Chan Santa Cruz hotel again. The next morning for breakfast, my dad and I met with an author named Mari Pintkowski who also owned a bed and breakfast with her husband near Tulum, about 45 minutes from Felipe Carrillo Puerto. Mari is from Colorado and wrote the book *Embarking on the Mariposa Trail.* Peissel's adventures on the Quintana Roo lost coast also fascinated her, so when I emailed her from Maine before we left, we quickly became friends. We met her for breakfast in Carrillo Puerto because she wanted to interview us about our walk and write some international online articles.

You can find these articles on the following websites: http://www.sac-be.com/footsteps_of_piessel.shtml, and http://www.sac-be.com/walking_part_two.shtml, http://www.sac-be.com/walking_part_3.shtml.

Luis, our trustworthy taxi driver, also met us for breakfast before he took us to the coast. After our interview and breakfast, we exchanged gifts and hugs before we said goodbye. So many people made our adventure memorable, and Mari is someone I will never forget. She made me feel like a celebrity during our interview, gave me advice on publishing this book, and became a kindred spirit who I felt connected to. As we said goodbye to Mari, she taught me a new Spanish phrase, "chippi chippi" rain. Chippi chippi means drizzling, and she hoped that the soft rain and cloudy skies would protect us from the relenting tropical sun as we continued our walk on the coast.

The rest of our one day in Carrillo Puerto was spent people-watching in the central park, riding the bicycles that Juan let us use around town, and eating barbecued chicken tacos at a small nameless diner for dinner. The light drizzle in the morning poured into warm tropical rain, which completely flooded the streets, but cooled off the entire town.

The next morning, Luis dropped us off near Punta Kanecahx, our last stop of the year. However, after we got out of the taxi, said our goodbyes, and started walking a couple of miles, we realized that we had passed the same run-down hurricane-ravaged resort that we walked by last year! Luis dropped us off too far north, so we were covering the same tracks as last year. We took a break underneath a makeshift metal roof with four posts stuck in the sand because of the heaven-sent chippi chippi while eating a snack and shaking our heads, laughing that, not only have we almost walked 600 miles, now we were retracing our steps! Oh, well. After our break, we went onwards and were delighted to be in new territory on our beloved coast, the light rain already cooling the sweat on our skin.

I thought these last 100 miles were the scariest because, as we got deeper into Southern Quintana Roo and the farthest from Cancún as one could be in Mexico, there were no people or occupied buildings around. Since we could only carry so many bottles of water, it was imperative that we find something on the beach with amenities, even a primitive dwelling. The beach was strewn with boulders and pebbles, making it hard to walk across. There was a small dirt road only a few yards from the beach. We decided walk on the road because it would make our travel much faster. This was a change of scenery for us because we could see the mangrove swamps. We had hoped to see crocodiles and other swamp creatures, but we did not see any. We only saw one car about every three to four hours. As four o'clock neared, it was time for us to start looking for a cabaña of some sort. We saw three local fishermen, but no cabañas.

The dilemma we faced had three possibilities: Do we sleep on the ground, ask the fishermen if they could drive us to a cabaña, sleep overnight and find someone to return us to the point we were at this time, or retrace our steps north to where we walked past some fishermen living in shacks? Regardless of our decision, we needed more water and food.

My dad sat on a log while we deliberated over our dilemma. We decided that we should talk to the fishermen to get information, and he made me talk while he rested on his log, probably knowing that they did not speak English, and his Spanish speaking skills were non-existent. Standing in the ocean, water up to their waists, the three fishermen cast their nets and poles. I took off my backpack, grabbed some paper pesos, and walked into the sea. They watched me as I waded gingerly through the water. I lost my balance from a small hole in the ocean floor, however, and I fell in, soaking myself and the pesos.

My dad guessed correctly. The fishermen did not speak English. I asked for the location of the nearest cabaña in broken Spanish. They replied that there were no cabañas on this coast. I then asked if they would bring us to Majahual in their car. Since this would have been hours of driving on the potholed dirt road, I could tell that they were not keen on this idea. Besides, there were no gas stations to be found, and who knew where the fishermen were from. Already embarrassed by my clumsiness, I said, "*Gracias*," and walked back to my dad, bringing him the bad news. With our unsuccessful idea, we decided to walk north, back to the sheds we saw, hoping to spend the night with some food and water. My dad swore he saw a woman with children at this shack. I was too frazzled and worried about being stranded to discuss any better ideas, so I agreed.

This would be the best idea he had while walking the whole 600 miles!

When we arrived around 5:00 pm, we desperately hoped that someone would take us in. We found the property, which consisted of about four thatched roofed shacks. A young pretty Mexican woman wearing a black tank top, and pink and white checkered capris lived there with three small children. Again, my dad made me deal with the locals while he hid in the beach grass. I approached and introduced myself.

She was friendly and responded in Spanish, "My name is Maria."

I explained our situation and asked in Spanish, "Could we rent out one of the sheds for the night?"

"Yes for 200 pesos, but I need to approve this with my husband when he returns from fishing." When I asked about a meal, she said, "I could serve a dinner of one fish to share for 9.00 USD, but there is no purified water." Their drinking water was from their concrete well, dug into the sand about 30 feet in depth and 5 feet in diameter.

Soon, Maria's husband arrived, and we found him pleasant since he agreed to let us stay for the night. But he was more reserved than his wife. We were shown to the shed and Maria started sweeping inside. Two other young adult male relatives and at least two dogs also lived with the family on this heavenly beach. The children were very curious about us strangers. I am sure that the family could not believe that we walked from Cancún to here!

The wooden shack we slept in was a fisherman's shed with the dimensions of 10 feet by 8 feet. Since it was the building closest to the water, it was directly in front of the surf. Inside the unfinished shed, we would each sleep in a reclining lawn chair made of canvas material with no mats underneath. There was an unfinished bathroom, but neither the sink nor the toilet was hooked up, and there was no running water. There was also no door to the outside that could be locked. The family left us alone in the shed while my dad and I sat down on the lawn chairs and thought about our predicament. However, I could still see the kids hanging around, hoping to catch a glimpse of our gear and our grimy faces.

My dad whispered, "Is it safe here? Will they take our money and throw us into the well?"

At this point, it was our only choice and the family seemed very genuine.

We walked outside, towards the family's eating area, which consisted of a white cracked plastic table with four chairs, set in the soft beach sand beside the kitchen. The outdoor kitchen was comprised of a wooden plank for a working area with a grill for cooking. Of course, there was no sink or running water. The whole set-up was almost like camping primitively in the United States. I wondered if this was how they lived all the time or whether this was their seasonal camp, too, and if they had a house in Majahual with a refrigerator, toilet, and running water.

We paid them for sleeping overnight and for the one meal. There was one more advantage in this situation. Since Maria's husband owned a motorized boat, he agreed to take us across Rio Hauch in the morning for an extra fee, solving our problem about not being able to walk across because of the burnt down bridge. Our dinner was served by Maria at the table in the sand. The fish was more than enough to share. The white, tender whole fish was fried to perfection, flaky and the freshest I have ever tasted. Hand-made tortillas, tomato and onion salsa, and lime were also served, so I made fish tacos.

As luck would have it, a pick-up truck appeared on the beach with groceries. We purchased two cold Crush orange sodas for one dollar. Apparently, this truck came once a week with a few groceries for the family to purchase. We ate heartily on the beach with this new family while the curious children hung around, taking in this odd but exciting moment with foreigners. Wanting to be social with Maria and help out, I offered to wash our dishes with her in their primitive outdoor kitchen.

My dad and I formed bonds with the kids since we were getting to know them through my broken Spanish, one word at a time.

I translated for my dad.

The children did not speak English at all. Their names were José, Leslie, and Alba, ages eight, five and three, respectively. Alba was a cute little girl with her big bright eyes and was shy, clinging to her mother and smiling while we were there. For the rest of the evening and the next morning, we played with José and Leslie. José wore a blue sports tank top, red shorts, and his demeanor showed he was very proud to be the big brother and protector. After dinner, his job was to fill the bucket from the well, so the camp could have fresh water. He was also very outgoing and seemed to like to learn new things. Leslie was also not shy, and she wore a pink tank top and yellow shorts.

My dad drew a hopscotch grid in the sand and taught them how to jump in the squares.

We then sat around the table, teaching them how to play tic tac toe and hangman on the blank pages in my dairy. I thought of small Spanish words for hangman, and they would guess it. Then, they discovered my electronic toys, the small Spanish-English dictionary and camera! Leslie was particularly curious and fond of the dictionary. She would punch in a word in Spanish and hit enter, so the word in English would come up, and she would show it to us. She used it as a way to communicate with us. She punched in the Spanish word *ñoña*, and the translation was whiny and fussy, and she smilingly pointed to her younger sister, Alba. We all laughed.

The next game of my father's was a big hit with all three of the kids, even Alba, and he called it "hide the toy game." The plastic table had a hole in the center for an umbrella. My dad found a small army man toy in the sand and, using a cup, would hide the toy underneath the cup and move it around the table. When the cup went over the hole, the toy would drop in the sand, so, when he picked up the cup, the army toy was nowhere to be found. The kids would giggle and move their hands for him to do it again and again.

After several times of hiding the toy, Leslie and José got bored, and they went swimming in the ocean. José was a protective big brother, holding up Leslie to help her swim while she floated on her stomach. Their father had laid out some kind of fish on the cutting table near the shore that Leslie motioned for me to come see. I was quite interested as the fish were strange looking; they had long spines, the body was about a foot in length and had small black, rusty brown, and white stripes. I later learned that these fish were named lionfish and had a fascinating story.

Red and common lionfish are not native to the Yucatán coast. Marine biologists speculate that they were bred in aquarium stores in Florida. When hurricane Andrew destroyed an aquarium in Southern Florida and the fish accidentally escaped, the lionfish had started to overtake the Mexican Caribbean. The aggressive venomous fish affect the food chain and the reef ecosystem by overpopulating and forcing native fish to less desirable environments.

The government is trying to stop the overrun of lionfish by conducting lionfish fishing derbies where whoever catches the most lionfish can earn 3,000.00 USD. I wonder if the fisherman knew that this species was invasive and wanted by the government. I also read that the lionfish was good for eating if filleted properly. Perhaps Maria's husband knew this and was going to prepare it for his family.

We also watched the children go about their daily lives with activities, like bathing in a large plastic blue tub that would fit Alba and Leslie at the same time. I took a picture of the three of them posing; Alba and Leslie were in the tub, and José was behind them, standing outside of the tub. Alba hid her face down in the tub. José drew the cool water from the well and filled up the tub, while one of his other relatives stood nearby. He took a bath by dumping a bucket of water over his head.

My dad, the kids, and I capped off the evening by looking at pictures from my home in Maine on my camera, and I read a children's book in Spanish with José. His parents and relatives were in the hut. Reading the book with José was special because it made me practice my Spanish pronunciations, and he was almost the same age as my son, Dylan.

We said goodnight to the family and retreated to our shed and lawn chairs. Of course, we had no blankets, pillows, or water to brush our teeth. It was a restless windy night on the beach. Since the unlatched front door was directly facing the ocean, it was chilly. The only covering I had for my legs was my paper thin wrap-around skirt. I piled the rest of my skimpy clothes into a pillow.

Upon waking at 5:30 am, after a nearly sleepless night, my dad and I contemplated what to do for breakfast and water for that day. But we were so tired that we were giddy, and our problems were soon forgotten as the morning turned into laughing sessions until it was time to go outside and greet the family. When we stepped out of our shed, the family had some wild coconuts ready for us to drink for breakfast. The coco water and soft meat would have to sustain us for the day's hike until we reached Costa de Cocos. As we drank, I gave José and Leslie my Maine postcards of snowy woods, animals, New England lobster cookouts and blueberry bushes. They accepted them and proudly showed their mother.

After our breakfast, the three men prepared the boat to take us across Rio Huach while we said our emotional goodbyes. My dad and I presented our loose pesos to the kids, so they could buy some candy the next time they went to Majahual. I often wonder, even today, if they are still in that particular spot on the deserted untamed beach in their simple thatched roof huts, and if they would remember us.

I called these experiences my National Geographic moment because of the cultural encounters and aspects. I knew that there must not be any gringos in the Cancún and Tulum areas that have shared the family's dinner of a whole fried fish, prepared in their rudimentary kitchen, spent an evening playing old fashioned games and reading with Mexican children, sleeping in their shed on hard chairs, and drinking wild coconut water for breakfast on a deserted beach.

I loved the boat rides along the open Caribbean Sea air, speeding past wild palm tree-lined beaches, which had been untouched by glamorous resort owners. This particular area of the coast was lined with mangroves. It was obviously a good idea that we had a boat since we could not walk over thick mangroves in swamps. We turned towards the mouth of the river and one of my favorite sights was a long stick with a torn purple and red cloth tied on the end, which marked the opening of the river. It looked like a post out of a Mark Twain book or pirate movie. As we entered the river, we saw the evidence of the burnt down bridge; blackened stumps stuck out of the water. Our captain, Maria's husband, gently guided us down the river to catch a glimpse of any crocodiles basking on the edge. Unfortunately, we did not see any.

Our National Geographic memories with the hospitable family ended as soon as the men dropped us off on the south shore and we waved goodbye.

We were alone in no man's land, with one bottle of water and no food, and I was the most scared that I had ever been. Since we did not know how far away Costa de Cocos in XCalak is and a source of drinking water was, we were entering a dangerous situation. This area was too remote to have accurate information.

So, we walked.

My dad's dreams of a clothing optional hotel on the other side of the river were crushed when we came upon abandoned wooden buildings that must have been the property of a thriving inn. I imagined parties, music blasting, beach volleyball games, and popular bars where the tourists in skimpy bathing suits waited in line to get cool margaritas and daiquiris. But we kept on walking more, disheartened, with miles to go on the tropical beach.

We did walk past a couple of private beach houses, where is where we desperately tried to get some drinking water, but no one was home. I was so distraught that I do not remember details of the houses, but they were probably worth millions, very neat, and colorful. I am sure they had some exotic frozen drinks that we could have had inside, or even some ice cold lemonade. We ended up sitting on their concrete steps, cooled by the shade, while I assessed my blisters. I had to cover them with band-aids and duct tape. How discouraging, to be sitting on the steps of this rich owner's luxury beach house and to be unable to get a cold drink!

I wanted to sit there for the rest of the day and night until the owner came home to rescue us, but my dad said we should keep walking and that we must be almost to Costa de Cocos!

After three to four hours of our grueling hike, the beach started to merge into mangrove swamps, so we used the dirt road. But that proved just as difficult with the bugs and lack of a breeze. We alternated between the beach, mangroves, and dirt road until finally the beach ran out. My guess was that we were getting closer to XCalak because the small town is bordered by Chetumal Bay, which leads to the Belize border. Usually, whenever we came upon a large body of water, it was bordered by swamps on one side instead of sandy beaches. We entered the jungle on a narrow path towards the dirt road. The path was so narrow that even our wide backpacks had trouble fitting through the thick brush.

Then, a scary situation surprised us on this jungle path.

In the middle of nowhere, a motorcycle had been parked on this path. It was completely out of place. My father was ahead, which really scared me. I had heard of all the Mexico drug violence and gang related gruesome murders. In that same year, a popular Club América soccer player, who was the leading goal scorer, was shot in the head in a bar by a mobster of the drug wars in Mexico City. The soccer player survived the attack. Even more disturbing, also in 2010, the Mexican cartel sewed the face of a 36 year old man on a soccer ball and left it in the streets of Sinaloa near the City Hall.

As my father was inching his way around the bike, trying not to knock it over, but barely getting through the jungle trees, I thought, "What in the world is this motorcycle doing parked in the jungle? What if there is some drug bust going on ahead that we are going to walk right into? Who would know we lay here at the end of our walk, dead, on this jungle path, in the middle of nowhere?" No one!

Half way around the bike, my dad ran into the supposed owner of the bike, walking the opposite way on the tight path. I think he was as shocked as us to come face-to-face with each other. Only pleasant exchanges took place, however, and I knew we were probably safe. Then, it was my turn to get around the bike and the owner, which I did cautiously.

After our ordeal in the jungle, we still did not know how far we need to walk to Costa de Cocos, but our landmark was an orange windmill that they used for electricity. I did not like walking on the road without the sea breezes of the beach, but it did offer us possible sightings of the cabaña's road signs, since that was how all the tourists arrived.

I was getting so desperate for something to drink, but in the afternoon, we sighted our orange windmill and the Costa de Cocos sign, the last place in Mexico.

As I dragged my sun burnt, rubbery legs up the steps to the bar and restaurant, one step at a time, I felt like I was dying of thirst. We plopped down in a seat and were served many cold drinks, so many that I lost count, and I had a feeling that the restaurant staff knew who we were and were expecting us. The staff also served us tuna fish sandwiches for lunch. It was only after having our fill that I took notice of my surroundings and realized that we made it! The bar and restaurant had an American Jimmy Buffett and fishermen's style. We were the only patrons there since it was off season, but I could picture a bunch of rowdy American fishermen coming here, year after year, to catch the biggest bonefish ever. I felt like I could find a place like this in Key West Florida. I felt safe and at home.

The property of Costa de Cocos had a volleyball court, and although there was no sandy beach, I imagined that the snorkeling was great offshore near the reefs. I knew that the Great Mayan Reef ran the length of the Yucatán to Belize, and since there were no waves at this inn, the sea was gentle and full of plant life and coral. Our bungalow was immaculate and the staff was friendly. There were two double beds and a hammock inside for lulling yourself to sleep with the tropical breezes that came through the windows. I loved this quaint XCalak pueblo and cabaña so much that I wanted to bring my family here someday.

During our short stay here, the gigantic land crabs fascinated me. I thought, "Wouldn't my son, or any other 10 year old adventurous boy, like to chase these crabs around the soft dirt around the property?" These land crabs have a body that is five to seven inches wide and are colored blue, rusty brown, and white, with huge bulging eyes. They reminded me of the movie *Eight Legged Freaks* because of the image of the creepy bodies and eight legs running towards the camera on the sand. I was curious to see what they would do if I came close to their homes, so I provoked the ugly crabs by stalking them. Eleven crabs came out of their holes in the dirt, charging right at me like an army. I ran away from them, looked back, and they were still coming at me.

We spent our evening at the inn, and the next morning, we made our arrangements to cross the border into San Pedro. The owner of Costa de Cocos instructed us to find the XCalak Harbormaster who would hook us up with a boat captain to take us to the Belize border. After an hour of searching for her around town, we found her at a neighbor's house, having coffee. We explained what we wanted and were relieved when she said she could help. She did not indicate that crossing the border into Belize territory, where there would be no official tourist crossing, would be a problem. It must have been a routine for Mexicans. She took us to her office, where we completed our Mexico exit documents, and hired a boat captain to take us into Belize and check us in. The office was typical of a government office, white from the ceiling to the tiled floor, with standard metal desks and no personal touches. Mexico newspapers littered the desks, displaying gruesome murders on the front page; this is routine in Mexican media reporting. The windows were duct taped in an X format for keeping hurricanes out. There were posters with the names of all hurricanes from the years 2005-2010 and the general ocean currents were also proudly displayed on the walls. I was fascinated by the Harbormaster's office since it reminded me of my good ol' Navy days. I asked if I could take the newspapers with me, to practice my Spanish, which the Harbormaster allowed.

Once our documents were in order and the captain was ready, we boarded an 18 foot utility motorized boat to make our way to Belize. Checking out of Mexico went smoothly, however, we still had to get into Belize. We were afraid of being turned away and sent back to Mexico where we came from, or of being told to enter Belize at the proper crossing. The boat ride across the Chetumal Bay was pleasant as usual because of the cool breezes on our sweaty skin, and I liked looking at the coastline and wondering if

I could explore that someday too—inspiring more adventures. Once we sighted Belize, I had a sad and heavy feeling in my stomach.

My beloved Mexico was out of sight, and our adventure was almost over.

Just like Peissel, we had no one at the border to cheer and congratulate us for walking from Cancún to Belize. I did not feel like jumping up and down out of excitement. Perhaps the thought of immigration dampened my spirits, or my intuition was telling me something.

We made our way to the docks in San Pedro, and the layout of the coast disappointed me. High rise hotels lined the shore, and most buildings resembled the buildings of a modern city. I was definitely not in Southern Quintana Roo anymore; I saw no cabañas with thatched roofs. My dad and I were grateful to our boat captain since he did all of the leg work and talked to the Belize Immigration and Customs officers. We did not end up in jail like Peissel. Although, I did take a picture while in the office to remember our momentous journey, which caused my dad to yell at me because taking pictures in an immigration office is illegal. That was the only alarming event that took place while entering Belize. Once our captain left us, and we wandered off to explore the Central American country. Our first order of business was to find good food, then we would check into a hotel, and walk Ambergris Cay.

The food was so bad that I do not even remember what we had that day—and now you know how much I like the food while traveling!

For breakfast one morning, I had a traditional Belizean food, which was a fried dough called fry jack, mushy eggs with no salsa, and runny beans. While my dad and I sat in our simple hotel, which overlooked San Pedro, I spread out my Belize money and passport, now stamped with Belize, on the bed to take pictures and prove that we made it. I still felt sad about leaving Mexico. But I knew there would be more adventures and perhaps I would come to love Belize and other Central American countries like I loved Mexico. So, we gathered our valuables and a day bag, and set off for the beach.

I immediately found out that the San Pedro area did not have a beach at all! And, as we walked north, there was still no beach! The coast was nothing but coral boulders and thick sea grass, with no sand and no gentle waves. It was not even close to being good for swimming. In addition, beggars who mothered five fatherless babies, tried to coax the tourists into giving them money. Disappointed, my dad and I walked inland to check out the back dirt roads and houses. We found an outside farmer's market, where I purchased a corn tamale, but found it too sweet. Our walk on the dirt roads brought us back to our hotel, and we decided to leave Ambergris Cay by ferry in the morning, interested in checking out Belize City and the rainforest inland. During our walk, we found a piece of land that was for sale, but it was flooded with muddy water, had a beat-up boat, and was not even one quarter of an acre.

I did not even like the music in Belize. They were playing Bryan Adams and Whitney Houston at one hotel. I like Whitney Houston, but when I am in the tropics, I want to hear tropical music, and it certainly was not Mariachi.

I had heard that Belize City had a high crime rate. One should not walk around the city in the daylight with a backpack because of thieves. So, we quickly went to the bus station and purchased two tickets to our destination of San Ignacio and the jungle lodge, Chaa Creek, about three hours away. The Blue Bird buses in Belize impressed me; it only cost 3.50 USD to go across the country to the Guatemalan border, but I was not impressed with the bus station; the floor was all mud. It certainly did not compare to the station in Felipe Carrillo Puerto. Although the buses do not run on time and have no air conditioning or movies, you cannot beat the price or the opportunity to mingle with the natives. While riding a Blue Bird bus, I thought our next adventure should be traveling Central America on a shoe string budget, again, making no reservations and traveling like the locals.

However, my intuition was right; I did not come to love Ambergris Cay or Belize City.

San Ignacio is located on the border of Guatemala. I was excited to explore a real rainforest and jungle once we left Belize City. I fell in love with the eco resort Chaa Creek for its natural lodge setting in the jungle among the Mayan Mountain Range. After checking into our tent cabin at the Macal River Camp, where we would stay for three days, my dad and I took the more difficult of the two ways to get to our cabin. We walked along a narrow rainforest medicine trail in the jungle, high above the Macal River, without a guide. Plants on the medicine trail included dysentery bark, cocoa bean trees, plants that decrease malaria and cleanse the blood vessels, and mangoes, breadfruit, limes and avocados. At one point on the trail, a ledge dropped about 600 feet and a tree leaned over the ledge. We had to hang onto the tree to swing over the ledge to get back to the trail again, with our backpacks on! Just walking on the slippery rocky trail with twisted vines and a heavy backpack was dangerous enough. The first time I did that, it was quite scary because I thought I would slip down the ravine, but since we had to do that each time we wanted to visit the swimming pool, main lodge, hike or kayak, I lost my fear.

Our tent cabin was simple, rustic and catered to outdoors people, like us, with no electricity, surrounded by nature. It had two small comfortable beds, with pillows and sheets, screens with curtains, and a porch with a hammock that faced the forest. I loved sleeping in the cabin, listening to the nighttime jungle sounds, just like the noises on a nature CD. The most exciting noise I heard in the jungle was a howler monkey at 2:00 am.

We were the only adventurers staying in the cabins, so we had our caretaker to ourselves and told our stories during our delicious meals, which were served under the thatched picnic area in the woods. Aside from us, two other unusual inhabitants dwelled in this camp and came out each morning to greet us: a gray fox and an agouti. During our stay, we did a few activities, including a canoe river journey on the Macal River, a hike on the rainforest trails near the Mayan horse stables and ruin mounds, and I took a jungle night hike.

Upon renting our canoe, I noticed that the canoe and life jackets were from Old Town Canoe, Incorporated, the company in Old Town, Maine!

Here we were, just finished walking from Cancún, Mexico to Belize, about to embark on a canoe journey, on a jungle river in Central America at Chaa Creek, which purchases the canoes from my current hometown near Bangor, Maine! After I got over my shock of seeing Old Town canoes, my dad thought we should take an inner tube with us to float back with the current. However, I was a little intimidated since this was a wild river in the jungle and I asked, "What about the snakes, fish with sharp teeth, like piranhas, crocodiles, and river iguanas?" I mumbled, "This is certainly not Maine where there are no poisonous creatures. The only harmful thing in a Maine river might be leeches."

His response was nonchalant. "There aren't any of those animals in the river—the staff said that there is a dam upstream, which keeps the large river iguanas from this part."

I had guessed that the staff was correct because we only saw water birds. However, the flora was spectacular, all shades of lush green. The misty rainforest, with mountains and caves, reminded me of ancient times. And the towering moss-covered trees inspired my imagination. I thought of how fun it would be to make a tree house like the Swiss Family Robinson. We paddled through the forest along a gentle current; as we floated past the caves, I imagined a Mayan Indian or Shaman stood there, watching us pass. On our way back, I decided to float on the inner tube for a small distance. Although it was scary, I did not get bit or stung, but once or twice, I felt something hit me from underneath.

We hiked some nature trails that afternoon, looking for ancient Mayan mounds in the forest. The air was heavy with humidity and part of the trail went up a steep, muddy and slippery slope. We found the mounds, but they were nothing but small hills in the jungle floor. The leaf cutter ants, who marched along the floor carrying leaves above their heads, interested me more. Their trail was obvious because it was a green line, as long as we could see, on our walking trail. It was the most amazing thing. The ants had intersections and they went straight into the woods, where their home must have been. I learned that the worker ants take the leaves underground where they live in a symbiotic relationship with fungus. They cultivate the fungus, their food source, by feeding the fungus leaves for the fungus to grow. The ants' underground nest can grow up to 98 feet.

I signed up for a jungle hike that night, and I was the only participant. My guide was 100% Mayan, 35 years old, and he also worked for the Belize military, hence his muscular frame, but he only stood about four and a half feet tall. He appeared to be in shape and strong, which made me feel secure. There was no way that I was going to walk around the jungle alone during the night without an experienced guide. My guide instructed me to strap my headlamp on my forehead and to stay close to him.

We started walking on the trail near the main lodge, but soon the filtered lights from Chaa Creek disappeared behind us and we entered the darkness of the jungle. The headlamp only allowed us to see directly in front of us. It provided enough light to keep me from tripping over the forest debris, but I could not see what lurked off the trail. The main trail had dewy grass on the sides, and my guide instructed me to shine my headlamp towards the grass.

I immediately saw thousands of tiny green fluorescent dots in the grass. I was amazed when he told me they were wolf spiders.

Later, I learned that wolf spiders have a toxic, painful bite. However, they control other harmful insect populations by eating them. Although my heart was pounding as we continued to walk, it was an exhilarating experience being so close to nature; my senses were heightened in the night.

At one point, all was quiet as we tiptoed along. I frantically looked in all directions for animals when, all of a sudden, there was a loud crash beside us in the brush. I must have jumped about three feet, then clung to the arm of my guide! He said it was probably a wild boar or armadillo, but I wondered if it was a jaguar. At the end of our walk, since my guide spoke perfect English, we chatted about each of our military experiences, and he told me that he is going to school to be a professional biologist and nature guide. It turned out to be a most memorable experience: a perfect end to this journey!

I saw a rainforest toad, kinkajou, Virginia opossum, tarantula, two types of scorpions, and wolf spiders. My favorite animals were the wolf spiders and tarantula.

On our last day, my dad and I talked our caretaker into giving us a ride to the nearest bus station, but first, he agreed to stop at the Xunantunich Mayan Ruins, only a few minutes away from camp. Before we left this area, I wanted to see large ancient Mayan ruins. The Xunantunich Mayan Ruins are located on the Guatemalan border. The only way to get to these ruins was by crossing a river on one of the last crank bridges in Central America on the Mopan River. The bridge was actually a "boat" connected to a cable that was secured on each river bank. The boat had a thin metal roof for protection from the sun, and planks of wood for the floor. The cable reached to the other side of the river and a winch cranked the cable back and forth, as we rode to the other side. The bridge employee let my dad crank the winch as our caretaker's truck was on the bridge going across the river.

There were many temples, tombs, and smaller pyramids on the property of Xunantunich. Along the way to the top of the main castle, there were lots of structures, temples, and rooms. A band of stucco decoration or frieze was on the very top. Archaeologists believe the ancient site probably had a city population of 7,000 to 10,000 inhabitants around 700 AD. The ruins served as a Mayan ceremonial center at that time. Xunantunich means 'stone maiden' in Mayan. According to the local legend, a maiden appeared one night in the 1890s, then disappeared into the stone. She wore a white dress and had red glowing eyes. My dad and I made the steep climb up the main castle at 130 feet before the tourists came that morning. At the top, we looked out over Guatemala and the lush green jungle. As our caretaker waited for us to explore the ruins and El Castillo, he told us later that he saw spider monkeys in the trees.

Our caretaker dropped my dad and me off at the bus station near the Guatemala border and, while we waited, I purchased some watermelon and pineapple from the local farmers. We made our trip back to Belize City, where we would stay overnight until it was time to catch our plane back to the United States in the morning. We needed to reach the airport, but it was many miles away. The hotel staff said the only way to get to the airport was by taxi for 25 USD. Of course, that did not sit well with my dad. He questioned, "How do *you* get to the airport?"

They repeated, "There is no other way to get to the airport other than by a taxi."

I foresaw another adventure coming out of these plans that my dad had to get us to the airport. Once we woke up the next morning, with plenty of time, he planned to walk out on the highway, with our backpacks and gear, in the direction of the airport, and to wave down a bus. Once we got on and confirmed that it was indeed going towards the airport, the cost was 1.50 USD!

But the problem was that the bus only dropped us off at the main intersection, so we had to walk at least two miles to the airport departures.

What were two miles, when we just walked 600 miles?

A Belize local got off the bus with us and introduced himself as someone who was also walking to work at the airport, and offered to let us walk with him so we would not get lost. He did not speak much English, but perhaps he spoke French. It was a long hot walk along the pavement near the fields and swamps. At one point, the airport employee said that a lot of crocodiles sometimes crowded those swamps. Then, I started thinking about the crime rate in Belize City and the fact that we are alone with this stranger on a deserted road near a swamp. But of course, the only things that happened were that we ended up hanging out with a local, making a new friend, and coming home to tell another story.

This concludes our adventures along the entire Yucatán coastline.

What started as a casual beach hike, ended as an international travel adventure, off-the-beaten-path, with my dad. Many of my dreams were realized – I challenged myself physically, learned a new culture and language, hiked beaches, set-up a fundraiser, slide show presentations, and a website, and wrote a book.

And, of course, I will always cherish the moments that I have shared with my dad.

CHAPTER 10

Thank you to the following people for helping us travel along the Mayan coast, from north to south:

• • •

The owner of Playa Los Pinos, for allowing us to cross his property for beach access on our first hike.

The staff at the Corona tents near Puerto Morelos, on the beach in the middle of nowhere, who gave us free cold drinks.

The three locals at the closed beach bar in Xpu Há, who opened coconuts for me and served coconut water over purified ice in a glass after a hot long hike.

The employees at the Que Onda hotel in Akumal and Hotel Acuario in Tulum who replenished my supply of bandaids for my blisters and gave me first aid for my back.

To the sailboat renters from Massachusettes in a deserted bay, who gave us ice cold beer even though I drank it too fast and injured my toe on coral after continuing to hike!

To all of the local fishermen that brought us across obstacles like the cliffs at Tulum, miles of mangroves, and Boca Paila.

To the construction workers in an abandoned hotel who gave us an endless supply of ice cold purified water when we needed it most.

To the employee at Cesiak tent cabins in the Sian Ka'an Bioreserve, who traveled to Tulum at night to buy me batteries because my camera didn't work.

To Ricky, the owner of the all-inclusive fishing lodge near Boca Paila, who allowed us to buy a delicious lunch of ham and cheese quesadillas. His cook also gave us free fruit to add to our backpacks!

To the employees at the all-inclusive resort near Akumal/Puerto Aventuras, who fed us a free breakfast at the bar when we were hungry, dirty, and sweaty. We had to beg for this one!

All of the tourists staying at all-inclusives from Puerto Morelos to Tulum that were able to sneak us water and food when we needed it.

A special appreciation to the picnicking Mexican family on the coast near Punta Allen that gave us a huge jug of purified water, ice and cups. It was well received as we were desperately thirsty for something cold.

A huge thank you to Lily from North Carolina, owner of Cuzan Guest House in Punta Allen for setting us up with Antonio the fisherman to take us across Acension Bay to the private island of Punta Pájaros.

Tom from Texas, the owner of Casa Blanca fishing lodge on this island. Thank you, Tom, for granting us permission to hike this private island, and for the guide and truck driver to the Tupak and Chac Mool ruins, as well as the delicious breakfast!

A special thank you to Gerardo, a guide at Palometa Club, who didn't know us, yet took us into his home in Punta Allen during Tropical Storm Arthur in 2008. He gave us Tom and Jerry and Superman towels to dry off, and shared a wealth of information about the coast, as well as seashells from his collection to bring back to the kids in Maine when I do my slide shows. And to Charlie, whose wife is from New Hampshire, for giving us a ride from Punta Allen to Tulum when my dad was sick.

To Marcia, the owner of Mayan Beach Garden near Placer, for sharing our story and the love of the book Lost World of Quintana Roo. As well as driving us north to hike this part of the coast and for the accurate information regarding the 2 miles of mangroves in Rio Indio.

To the friendly dog that shared our hike and trail for 2 hours! Great companion!

To the Spanish-speaking-only local that opened a wild coconut for me when I did not have my machete.

And lastly, a special thank you for the local taxista, Luis, in Felipe Carillo Puerto for introducing us to a Mayan cultural show, and taking us to the coast so we can continue to hike when the local bus was not available.

Also, I want to thank you and your brother for taking us to a remote cenote not visited by tourists when no other taxistas could find one and to the local swimming pool fed by a cenote in Felipe Carillo Puerto to cool off.

Made in the USA
Columbia, SC
03 November 2018